Shakespeare Problems

Also from Westphalia Press
westphaliapress.org

The Idea of the Digital University

Dialogue in the Roman-Greco World

The History of Photography

International or Local Ownership?: Security Sector Development in Post-Independent Kosovo

Lankes, His Woodcut Bookplates

Opportunity and Horatio Alger

The Role of Theory in Policy Analysis

The Little Confectioner

Non Profit Organizations and Disaster

The Idea of Neoliberalism: The Emperor Has Threadbare Contemporary Clothes

Social Satire and the Modern Novel

Ukraine vs. Russia: Revolution, Democracy and War: Selected Articles and Blogs, 2010-2016

James Martineau and Rebuilding Theology

A Strategy for Implementing the Reconciliation Process

Issues in Maritime Cyber Security

A Different Dimension: Reflections on the History of Transpersonal Thought

Iran: Who Is Really In Charge?

Contracting, Logistics, Reverse Logistics: The Project, Program and Portfolio Approach

Unworkable Conservatism: Small Government, Freemarkets, and Impracticality

Springfield: The Novel

Lariats and Lassos

Ongoing Issues in Georgian Policy and Public Administration

Growing Inequality: Bridging Complex Systems, Population Health and Health Disparities

Designing, Adapting, Strategizing in Online Education

Pacific Hurtgen: The American Army in Northern Luzon, 1945

Natural Gas as an Instrument of Russian State Power

New Frontiers in Criminology

Feeding the Global South

Beijing Express: How to Understand New China

The Rise of the Book Plate: An Exemplative of the Art

Shakespeare Problems

Shakespeare's Fight with the
Pirates and the Problems of the
Transmission of his Text

---

by Alfred W. Pollard

WESTPHALIA PRESS
An Imprint of Policy Studies Organization

Shakespeare Problems: Shakespeare's Fight with the Pirates and the Problems
of the Transmission of his Text
All Rights Reserved © 2018 by Policy Studies Organization

Westphalia Press
An imprint of Policy Studies Organization
1527 New Hampshire Ave., NW
Washington, D.C. 20036
info@ipsonet.org

ISBN-13: 978-1-63391-645-6
ISBN-10: 1-63391-645-6

Cover design by Jeffrey Barnes:
jbarnesbook.design

Daniel Gutierrez-Sandoval, Executive Director
PSO and Westphalia Press

Updated material and comments on this edition
can be found at the Westphalia Press website:
www.westphaliapress.org

SHAKESPEARE PROBLEMS
By A. W. POLLARD & J. DOVER WILSON

SHAKESPEARE'S FIGHT WITH
THE PIRATES AND THE
PROBLEMS OF THE
TRANSMISSION
OF HIS TEXT

CAMBRIDGE UNIVERSITY PRESS
C. F. CLAY, Manager
LONDON: FETTER LANE, E.C. 4

NEW YORK : THE MACMILLAN CO.
BOMBAY
CALCUTTA } MACMILLAN AND CO., Ltd.
MADRAS
TORONTO : THE MACMILLAN CO. OF
CANADA, Ltd.
TOKYO : MARUZEN-KABUSHIKI-KAISHA

ALL RIGHTS RESERVED

SHAKESPEARE'S FIGHT WITH THE PIRATES AND THE PROBLEMS OF THE TRANSMISSION OF HIS TEXT

BY

ALFRED W. POLLARD

SANDARS READER IN BIBLIOGRAPHY

1915

SECOND EDITION, REVISED

WITH AN INTRODUCTION

CAMBRIDGE

AT THE UNIVERSITY PRESS

1920

CONTENTS

	PAGE
INTRODUCTION	vii
THE REGULATION OF THE BOOK TRADE IN THE SIXTEENTH CENTURY	1
AUTHORS, PLAYERS AND PIRATES IN SHAKESPEARE'S DAY	26
THE MANUSCRIPTS OF SHAKESPEARE'S PLAYS	53
THE IMPROVERS OF SHAKESPEARE	81
INDEX	105

INTRODUCTION

THE lectures here reprinted were delivered in November, 1915, in the University of Cambridge, under the terms of the Sandars Readership in Bibliography. They were printed in successive numbers of *The Library* in 1916, and published in book-form the following year. Thanks largely to a friendly controversy which followed a generous review in the *Literary Supplement* of *The Times*, the small first edition was speedily exhausted, and the book has been for some time out of print. That a new edition of it is offered here as the first volume of the series of monographs on *Shakespeare Problems* projected by Mr Dover Wilson and myself is due partly to my desire that the lectures should reappear under the auspices of the Press of the University which honoured me with the invitation to deliver them, partly to their forming the starting point from which most of the Problems with which this series is concerned will be approached. The central idea of the lectures is that the early editions upon which a text of Shakespeare's plays must be built, are a good deal closer to the original manuscripts from his pen than most of the text-builders have allowed. In the subsequent volumes of this series Mr Dover Wilson and I hope to show that because the text-builders have underrated their sources they have neglected many of the clues which these offer, and that the clues lead to very interesting results, also that the futility of many of the 'conjectural emendations' which overload the

Variorum editions is amply accounted for by the neglect of their venturesome authors to take any account of the character of the hand in which the plays were written. In many respects, if we are to do better, we must make a fresh start.

Some apology is perhaps needed for one who has already written, or helped in writing, four books on Shakespeare bibliography, now taking part in planning a new series of booklets on the same subject. The best plea in mitigation that can be offered is that one bit of work has led to another, often with the help of an idea borrowed from a friend, and that in a research so largely new it is only by taking one step at a time that any sure progress can be made. One or two points have, I hope, been definitely cleared up and the elucidation of these has revealed pathways of advance which previously could hardly have been distinguished.

The first of these points is as to the editions of *The Merchant of Venice*, Printed by J. Roberts, 1600; *A Midsummer Night's Dream*, Printed by Iames Roberts, 1600; *King Lear*, Printed for Nathaniel Butter, 1608; and *Henry V*, Printed by T. P., 1608. As long as these imprints and dates were accepted as correct, it was impossible to arrive at any sound conception of the Shakespeare Quartos as a class, or of the part played by James Roberts in their publication. Accident having brought under my notice, at an interval of three or four years, first a volume belonging to Edward Gwynn (a seventeenth century collector) and then, in 1906, one owned by Mr Hussey, each containing these four plays with six others[1]

---

[1] *The Whole Contention between the two Famous Houses, Lancaster and York*, Printed for T. P , n.d., in two parts, counting

INTRODUCTION ix

(three of them dated 1619) by or attributed to Shakespeare, I was led to look for traces of other volumes made up in the same way, and finding clear proof that Garrick and Capell[1] had both owned such volumes leapt at the conclusion that in 1619 advantage was taken of the issue of reprints of *The Merry Wives of Windsor*, *Pericles* and the *Yorkshire Tragedy*, to bind up with them the unsold stock of earlier editions. The theory was set forth in an article contributed to *The Academy* (2nd June, 1906) entitled *Shakespeare in the Remainder Market*. Two years later, I had the pleasure of printing in *The Library* (2nd Series, vol. IX. pp. 113-131) an article by Dr W. W. Greg, *On Certain False Dates in Shakespearian Quartos*, which drew attention to the "curious similarity of style in the various titlepages" of the plays in the volume of 1619 which I had supposed to have been made up of new editions and remainders, to the use in them of large numerals not elsewhere found before 1610, and of devices followed by Roberts' imprint which Roberts is not known to have used, also (and chiefly) to the evidence offered by the watermarks that "the whole volume is printed on one mixed stock of paper," which "could not have been the case if the individual plays had been printed

as two: *Pericles, Prince of Tyre*, Printed for T. P., 1619; *The first part of the Life of Sir John Old-castle*, Printed for T. P., 1600; *The Merry Wives of Windsor*, Printed for Arthur Johnson, 1619; *A Yorkshire Tragedie*, Printed for T. P., 1619.

[1] Later research suggests that the copies of the ten plays owned by Dr Farmer, the Duke of Roxburghe, Thomas Jefferson and T. P. Barton, had originally belonged to similar volumes. See *A Census of Shakespeare Quartos*, by H.C. Bartlett and A. W. Pollard, Yale University Press, 1916, Introduction, pp. xxvii *sqq.*

INTRODUCTION

at different dates extending over a period of twenty years." Dr Greg quite rightly deduced from this evidence that all the editions in the 'Gwynn' volume were printed together in 1619. He thus at a blow rid literary criticism and bibliography of the problems falsely raised by what had been taken to be duplicate editions of those of *The Merchant of Venice* and *A Midsummer Night's Dream*, rightly dated 1600, and of *King Lear*, rightly dated 1608.

Dr Greg's contention won considerable acceptance, but the argument from non-occurrence used in the case of the large numerals and the devices is necessarily weak, while the proof (for such it was) from watermarks embedded in the backs of small quartos often tightly bound was not easily checked. The following year Mr William Jaggard helped, by showing in *The Library* (2nd Series, vol. IX. pp. 208–11) that his ancestor, both before and after 1619, was using papers with watermarks similar to those found in the plays in the Gwynn volume. In chapter IV. of my *Shakespeare Folios and Quartos* (written as an introduction to Messrs Methuen's excellent series of facsimiles of the four Shakespeare Folios) I added arguments from the text-type used in *The Merchant of Venice* and other plays, from the spelling and other points. There was growing assent, but in *The Library* for January, 1910 (3rd Series, vol. I. pp. 36–45) in an article *On the Supposed False Dates in certain Shakespeare Quartos*, Mr Alfred Huth defended my original hypothesis of a 'remainder volume' as against Dr Greg's of false dates with equal courtesy and skill, and though I bowled my hardest against him I am not sure that any umpire, still less the average bookman, would have granted that I bowled

INTRODUCTION xi

him out. Before the year closed, however, Mr William Neidig, an instructor in the University of Wisconsin, in two articles in American reviews[1] offered a physical proof which could not be gainsaid. Having first obtained exact photographic facsimiles of all the title-pages in question (photographing a millimetre rule along with each so as to enable its accuracy to be tested),

"He then plotted out each title-page into little squares, and by this means convinced himself that the words 'Written by W. Shakespeare,' the 'Heb Ddieu, Heb Ddim' device, and the word 'Printed' in the title-page of 'Pericles' dated 1619, and of the 'Merchant of Venice' dated 1600, come in precisely the same places, and demonstrated this beyond possibility of cavil by a composite photograph in which the 'Merchant of Venice' is superimposed on 'Pericles,' and the words in question come out quite sharply, and the device with only the very slightest blur, showing that the block may have been shifted a fraction of a millimetre. The occurrence in both title-pages of an identical flaw of one kind in the W of 'Written' and of another kind in the W of Shakespeare's initial, completes the proof that this portion of the title-page of 'Pericles' had been used again in the title-page of the 'Merchant of Venice' and thus offered a pretty demonstration of the impossibility of their having been separated by an interval of nineteen years. Mr Neidig thinks that the trouble-saving printer 'lifted off the lower portion' of one title-page for use in another. It

---

[1] *Modern Philology*, October, 1910 (pp. 1–19, 'The Shakespeare Quartos of 1619'), and *The Century Magazine*, October, 1910 (pp. 912–919, 'False Dates on Shakespeare Quartos').

seems to me more probable that he picked out all the rest of the contents of the forme, rather than risked dropping out letters by transferring the old matter to a new one; but that the same type-letters in the same setting-up were used in the 'Yorkshire Tragedy' of 1619, 'Pericles' of 1619, 'Merchant of Venice' of 1600, and 'Merry Wives' of 1619, he has proved up to the hilt; and I think that henceforth any bookseller who sells the '1600' 'Merchant of Venice' as printed in that year, will be liable to have it returned[1]."

Possibly because of the hint in this last paragraph, the editions in question are now, I believe, always sold with a mention of the spuriousness of their dates, so that at least this one problem may be considered definitely settled. To the literary student the most important result is the disappearance of all theories as to the true and false editions bearing the same dates being printed from different manuscripts, and also of the contention, which had been generally accepted, that the falsely dated *Merchant of Venice* was the true

[1] From my review of Mr Neidig's articles in *The Library* (3rd Series, vol. II. pp. 101-107) for January, 1911. In the same review I mentioned a curious fact, to which my attention had first been called by Mr E. H. Dring, viz. that in copies of the falsely-dated issues the dates have sometimes been torn away in a manner which points to deliberate intent. This suggests that when Laurence Heyes reasserted his claim to his father's copyright at Stationers' Hall, on 8th July, 1619, the false dates, having been adjudged spurious, were mutilated by way of penalty, enforced either by the Company or by private agreement. While the volume may originally have been planned honestly, there seems little room for doubt that before it was completed a deliberate attempt had been made to 'wangle' the copyrights of the *Merchant of Venice* and *Midsummer Night's Dream*.

INTRODUCTION xiii

'first edition.' To bibliographers, on the other hand, the chief gain was the solution of the difficulties as to Roberts' use of his types and the reversal of the current view of him as the most daring of the pirates who attacked the property of the players. It became possible to understand his entries in the Stationers' Register as 'staying' entries, made in the interests of the actors to render piracy more difficult, a rôle which accorded much better with his position as holder of a privilege for printing all play-bills than the predatory career usually assigned to him.

Read by this new light on Roberts' career, the entries in the Stationers' Register become intelligible and there was the less reason to believe that the Company had grossly abused the powers entrusted to it to the detriment of authors. In writing my *Shakespeare Folios and Quartos* in 1909, I gave the Stationers credit for the moderate degree of honesty which succeeds in maintaining itself when times are not too hard, and the players for the moderate power of self-defence which, when one horse has been stolen from a stable in which others are still kept, sets about getting a new lock for the stable-door. As I then wrote:

"The theory that anyone could steal and print an Elizabethan play and obtain copyright in it by paying sixpence to the Stationers' Company, to the exclusion of the author and his assigns, does not conflict with the official functions either of the Censors of the Press or of the Stationers' Company. Neither the one nor the other were legally bound to show any consideration to authors. What the theory, when extended to cover not an isolated instance but a whole series of depredations, conflicts with, is common sense and the English character. It is understood that in this happy land if various people did all the things they are legally entitled to do, the Constitution would be in a sad plight. But these mysterious possibilities remain unfulfilled, and while they are unfulfilled, no one troubles to obtain paper guarantees against them, with the result that future historians will perhaps gravely argue that of course they happened."

Historians of the drama had argued with great gravity that all the publishers of Shakespeare's plays were thieves, and that the Stationers' Company was always on the side of the thief. The main work of my *Shakespeare Folios and Quartos* was the demonstration that the more charitable view (that while some publishers were thieves others were honest, and that the Stationers' Company, as a body, when called on to lend its help to one side or the other, at least occasionally is found helping the right man) explains alike the reference to 'stolne and surreptitious copies' in the Address to the Reader in the First Folio and the entries in the Register much more successfully than the pessimism which had become traditional with the writers on Shakespeare's text. When the available data were interpreted on these lines the early quartos fell into two groups: (i) of four bad texts to which alone the epithets 'stolne and surreptitious' properly applied, viz. *Romeo and Juliet*, 1597, *Henry V*, 1600, *The Merry Wives of Windsor*, 1602, and *Hamlet*, 1603, all entered irregularly on the Stationers' Register or not at all, with *Pericles*, 1609, as a later instance of a similar kind; and (ii) of fourteen (positively or comparatively) good texts, twelve of which were regularly entered on the Register, while

INTRODUCTION

of the other two one certainly (*Romeo and Juliet*, 1599) and the other probably (*Loves Labors Lost*) were printed to take the place of copies rightly called 'stolne and surreptitious.' The chapters devoted to this topic in the *Shakespeare Folios and Quartos* book were written controversially and on some minor points did not make the best of their case. In the first and second of these Sandars Lectures, the argument is put as well as I can put it, and it has not yet been challenged.

Between the writing of the *Shakespeare Folios and Quartos* of 1909 and the Sandars Lectures of 1915, a little book was published, Mr Percy Simpson's *Shakespearian Punctuation* (Oxford, at the Clarendon Press, 1911, pp. 107, price 5s.), which was a real inspiration to me, none the less so because I put my own interpretation on some of the facts which I owed to Mr Simpson. Mr Simpson's main thesis was that the punctuation which is usually regarded as the weakest point in the printing of the Folio of 1623, is "on the whole sound and reasonable." He asked "was there, or was there not, a system of punctuation which old printers used," and proved conclusively that there was such a system and that numerous pointings in the First Folio which ignore our modern (not very successful) rules for applying a logically appropriate pointing to every grammatical construction, when interpreted on the lines of the older system are strikingly justified. Something is said of Mr Simpson's book in the fourth of these lectures, but before this was delivered I had already written more fully on the subject in the introduction to *A New Shakespeare Quarto, the Tragedy of King Richard II, printed for the third time by Valentine Simmes in*

INTRODUCTION

1598[1], in which I had more space at my disposal. To have enlarged what I wrote for my lecture would have destroyed its balance, and I may therefore be pardoned for quoting a few paragraphs from my *Richard II* introduction to illustrate the importance of the new light I owed to Mr Simpson in dealing with the Quartos, with which his own little book was not concerned.

Mr Simpson's two points as regards the old punctuation were (i) that "the earlier system was mainly rhythmical" rather than logical, and (ii) that whereas "modern punctuation is uniform; the old punctuation was quite the reverse," and that this 'flexible' system of punctuation enabled poets to "express subtle differences of tone." Commenting on this, I wrote:

"In plays, wherever punctuation becomes important, it might perhaps best be called 'dramatic.' To get at its underlying principle we may go back to the lessons of the schoolroom in which I learnt that, when a comma stopped the way, I must pause while I could count one; when a semicolon, while I could count two; when a colon, three; when a full-stop, four. Educational formulas are long-lived, and it is possible that this simple rule of thumb, which made each stop simply and solely a measure of time, came down from Elizabethan days. It is certainly quite inapplicable to modern punctuation. Anyone who read aloud and marked his stops like this would risk having things thrown at him. In reading aloud we ignore many of the stops with which

[1] Reproduced in facsimile from the unique copy in the library of William Augustus White. With an introduction by Alfred W. Pollard. Bernard Quaritch, 1916.

grammarians have taught printers to pepper our pages. The stops may sometimes save us from mistaking the sense, but they give hardly any clue as to how a given passage should be 'taken,' and it is precisely this which the punctuation of the First Folio attempted to do—and, at least occasionally, did.

"The strength of Mr Simpson's treatise lies in his examples, and the example which effected my conversion was a line and a half from *King Henry V* (V. i. 49 *sq.*) spoken by Pistol as, in terror of Fluellen's cudgel, he begins to eat the leek. In the Folio it is printed, quite shamelessly:

> By this Leeke, I will most horribly reuenge I eate and eate I sweare.

In the Globe Shakespeare there is a colon after 'reuenge' and a comma after the second 'eate'; but the Folio shows us Fluellen flourishing his cudgel, and how should Pistol stop while he might count three after 'reuenge,' or even one after 'eate,' when the slightest pause might bring the cudgel on his head? The absence of stops here can hardly be called rhythmical, but it is certainly dramatic, and it gives what is practically a stage direction, which is totally lacking in the modern rendering.

"While I was pondering this section chance brought to me, at second hand[1], a delightful piece of Shakespearian punctuation of an opposite kind, in Mr Anstey's *Voces Populi*. A Hyde Park orator is

---

[1] In a quotation in the Rev. Cyril A. Alington's *A Schoolmaster's Apology* (Longmans, 1914).

giving his views on ministerial shortcomings, and by printing his observations as:

The present Government Har. The most Abandoned! The most Degraded! The most Cowardly! The most Debased! The most Ber-lud-thirsty! Set. Of Sneakin' Ruffians. That hever disgraced the Title. Of so-called Yumanity

Mr Anstey not only tells us exactly what his orator said, but exactly how he said it. Here, in fact, we have the First Folio punctuation in a nut-shell, emphasis-capitals and all."

Mr Simpson had concerned himself only with the punctuation of the Folio. In my introduction to the facsimile of the newly identified quarto of *Richard II* I was trying to follow the transmission of the text of one of the 'good' Shakespeare Quartos from the time when the ink first dried on Shakespeare's manuscript of it to the publication of the first Quarto in 1597 and again on from that till the pages on which it is printed in the First Folio were finally printed off. I could not help believing that the punctuation, or lack of punctuation, in Pistol's line and a half represented exactly how that line and a half was 'taken' when *Henry V* was performed at the Globe, and I did not doubt that it also represented exactly how the line and a half was written in Shakespeare's original manuscript. Were there any passages in the first quarto of *Richard II* for which as much as this could be claimed?

In writing this last sentence, I have unconsciously allowed experience to modify my question. There was a brief excited moment during which it took the larger form, 'Was the first Quarto of *Richard II* punctuated throughout like this'? To that an honest editor can

INTRODUCTION

only return one answer: 'In any positive sense it was *not*.' Negatively and defectively we may persuade ourselves that its light, inadequate punctuation corresponds roughly to what Shakespeare set down, but for pages at a time there is nothing on which we can put our finger and say 'that punctuation must be Shakespeare's.' On the other hand, as regards the set speeches, and now and again elsewhere, the punctuation is distinctly dramatic and entitles us to believe that Shakespeare punctuated these portions of his manuscript with some care and that the Quarto reproduces this punctuation with very much the same substantial fidelity that it reproduces the words of the text.

"In the Cambridge edition, lines I. i. 92–100 are thus printed:

> Besides I say and will in battle prove,
> Or here or elsewhere to the furthest verge
> That ever was survey'd by English eye,
> That all the treasons for these eighteen years   95
> Complotted and contrived in this land
> Fetch from false Mowbray their first head and spring.
> Further I say, and further will maintain
> Upon his bad life to make all this good,
> That he did plot the Duke of Gloucester's death...

Plump at the end of l. 96, separating 'treasons' from its verb, the Quarto inserts a colon, and the line "Fetch from false Mowbray their first head and spring" comes rushing out after the pause with doubled effect. And at the end of this line, shade of Lindley Murray! there is no full stop—only a comma; for Bolingbroke will not give Mowbray a chance to interrupt him, but dashes on with his second accusation, with only an imperceptible pause. In the earlier lines, on the other hand, when he is preparing the way for his rush, Bolingbroke's measured tones are marked by two stops which the Cambridge editors omit, a comma after 'say' in l. 92, and another after 'here' in the next line. Grammatically a comma after 'here' should entail another after 'elsewhere,' but dramatic punctuation sets no store on pairing its commas and usually omits either one or the other."

That the punctuation in this passage is no mere accident to which a fanciful interpretation has been assigned, may be shown by quoting another set speech from the same source. As a rule Richard is exhibited in the Quarto as a rapid speaker, seldom needing a heavier stop than a comma, and the contrast to his usual style which we find in his despondent speech, III. iii. 142–159, when he finds himself obliged to speak Bolingbroke fair is marked in the first Quarto by a punctuation obviously deliberate. In this text it reads:

> What muſt the King do now? muſt he ſubmit?
> The King ſhall do it: muſt he be depoſde?
> The king ſhall be contented: muſt he looſe
> The name of King? a Gods name let it go:
> Ile giue my iewels for a ſet of Beades:
> My gorgeous pallace for a hermitage:
> My gay apparel for an almeſmans gowne:
> My figurde goblets for a diſh of wood:
> My ſcepter for a Palmers walking ſtaffe:
> My ſubiects for a paire of carued Saintes,
> And my large kingdome for a little graue,
> A little little graue, an obſcure graue,
> Or Ile be buried in the Kings hie way,
> Some way of common trade, where ſubiects feete
> May hourely trample on their foueraignes head;
> For on my heart they treade now whilſt I liue:
> And buried once, why not vpon my head?

INTRODUCTION xxi

Here the Cambridge editors check the passion of the cry 'a God's name let it go' by a comma after 'name'; substitute commas for colons at the end of the next five lines, and on the other hand put a semicolon after 'an obscure graue' instead of a comma and again another semicolon instead of a colon after 'liue.' By these changes in the time in which the several sections of the speech are taken the whole passage is reduced, as far as the words allow, to a dull monotony. The punctuation of the first Quarto, on the other hand, accents the despondent slowness of the beginning, the swiftness of the cry of impatience and the pauses between the meditative lines in which Richard soothes himself with his fancies. Then at the idea of death it shows him swept away by a flood of self-pity, which will bear no stops heavier than commas till it slows down for the final reproach, and (after a long pause) the sombre sarcasm which succeeds it. No printer could have invented this exquisitely varied punctuation. Is there any room for doubt that it gives the lines as Shakespeare trained his fellows to deliver them? Is there any greater room for doubt that it gives us the lines as Shakespeare punctuated them himself as he wrote them down while he heard the accents in which Richard, as he conceived him, was to speak them? These colons and commas take us straight into the room in which *Richard II* was written and we look over Shakespeare's shoulder as he penned it.

When I wrote my *Shakespeare Folios and Quartos*, I wrote as a bibliographer and a lover of logical economy impatient of hypotheses disproportionately large compared with the facts they were framed to explain, also as an optimist impatient of the pessimism

INTRODUCTION

which represents human nature as worse than it is. For a quarter of a century my work had brought me into touch with printers and publishers and editors, and I stood up for my friends. I satisfied myself that most of the Quartos were not 'stolne and surreptitious,' that the Folio editors made no use of the four that were, and that in other respects they did fairly well. I owe it to Mr Simpson's little book and to Mr W. A. White who exhorted me to put all I could into the introduction to the facsimile of his newly-found Quarto[1] that I woke up at last to the fact that I was playing for much higher stakes than I had in the least realized, that here was evidence which concerned not merely the good name of Roberts or Heminge and Condell, or Blount, but the whole problem of the transmission of Shakespeare's text, with possibilities of finding ourselves in an actual contact with him of which I had previously not allowed myself to dream. My hopes rose higher when in gathering materials for my third Sandars lecture I found myself able to show (1) that many of Shakespeare's plays were printed from prompt copies and (2) that some plays by other writers which have come down to us in manuscript are autographs to which the prompter had added his notes. There was room, as I ought to have emphasized, for a copyist of almost photographic fidelity between the prompt copy and the printed texts, but a copyist making a copy for printing would surely have edited away the more obvious prompter's notes. In any case the link I sought to establish holds fast to this extent that no one who knows the evidence can say it is impossible, or

[1] Also to Miss Henrietta Bartlett who generously waived in my favour her claim as the discoverer to edit it herself.

INTRODUCTION   xxiii

even very improbable, that some of the copy used in printing both the good Quartos and the Folios was actually in Shakespeare's autograph. If we honestly admit this possibility it must alter our whole attitude to the extant texts.

Shakespeare died in 1616, and out of the commemoration, maimed by the occurrence of the tercentenary in the middle of the Great War, came Sir Edward Maunde Thompson's book on *Shakespeare's Handwriting* (Oxford, at the Clarendon Press, 1916) which showed by a masterly analysis that Shakespeare must have written a hand of the same style as that found in the three pages of the extant manuscript of the play of *Sir Thomas More* (British Museum Harleian MS. 7368) in which More persuades the May-day rioters to submission. I believe myself that my old Chief's full claim that those three pages are the work of Shakespeare and written by him with his own hand is well founded and will ultimately be accepted by all competent judges, as it has been already by the few who are familiar with the manuscript. It is proposed that one of the volumes of our Shakespeare Problems series should deal with this question. But splendid as is the hope of finding ourselves in acknowledged possession of three pages in Shakespeare's autograph, the gain of having secured the guidance of a great expert in translating for us the six authentic signatures (written, one of them with obvious impatience, two with the uncertainty as to what they ought to do which comes over laymen when they have to sign important documents in the presence of a lawyer, and three in sickness) into the hand in which the plays were written in the abounding vitality of the prime of life is potentially even greater. We now know at least approximately the rules to which the emendation of Shakespeare must conform if it is to be anything better than a game of literary guess-work. Ninety-nine per cent. of the shots which overcrowd the notes of the Variorum editions are shown to be altogether off the target, and the way is prepared for a saner class of emendations, wholesomely limited by the condition that in an Elizabethan English hand they must look sufficiently like what appears in the printed texts for it to be conceivable that a scribe or printer should have mistaken the one for the other.

This willing submission to limitations recognized as the rules of what, being Englishmen, we shall probably call 'the game,' has a very important counterpart and also applies to other editings besides those which involve the substitution of one or more words for others. As an example of its extension we may take the line-arrangements, which should not lightly be altered unless we can see how and why the scribe or printer went wrong. Its counterpart lies in the necessity of refusing to be satisfied with merely setting right an obvious error until we have discovered what lies behind it. Faced with the double disarrangement of the lines in Theseus' speech in the *Midsummer Night's Dream* (V. i. 1–20) here printed from Fisher's Quarto of 1600, previous critics of Shakespeare's text had contented themselves with the easy task of rearranging as four the first three italicized lines in the passage as here printed, and the five and a quarter as six, in accordance with the slanting strokes here inserted:

Hip. Tis strange, my Theseus, that these louers speake of.
The. More straunge then true. I neuer may beleeue

INTRODUCTION

These antique fables, nor these Fairy toyes.
Louers, and mad men haue such seething braines,
Such shaping phantasies, that apprehend | more,
Then coole reason euer comprehends. | The lunatick
The louer, and the Poet | are of imagination all compact. |
One sees more deuils, then vast hell can holde:
That is the mad man. The louer, all as frantick,
Sees Helens beauty in a brow of Ægypt.
The Poets eye, in a fine frenzy, rolling, | doth glance
From heauen to earth, from earth to heauen. | And as
Imagination bodies forth | the formes of things
Vnknowne: the Poets penne | turnes them to shapes,
And giues to ayery nothing, | a locall habitation,
And a name. | Such trickes hath strong imagination,
That if it would but apprehend some ioy,
It comprehends some bringer of that ioy.
Or in the night, imagining some feare,
How easie is a bush suppos'd a Beare?

Mr Dover Wilson was not so easily contented. He could not believe that if the copy which the scribe or the printer had before him had arranged the lines correctly it would not have been faithfully followed. Nor did he rush at the explanation, too readily offered in such cases, that the printer had no copy before him, but was setting up his lines at the dictation of some extraordinarily leisured person who read out the text at the rate of a line a minute, the quickest possible rate at which it could be set in type. He noticed that the lines here printed in roman letter are concerned only with lovers and madmen; those in italic not only with lunatics and lovers, but also with 'the poet,' and so reached the conclusion that the italicized lines were an afterthought, written, in such space as could be found, on the margin, and transferred thence to the text by a scribe or printer who had no instinct for dividing them rightly. Thus we can look over Shakespeare's shoulder, not only when he is in the first heat of inspiration, but also when he is revising, though in truth in this case he seems to have been better inspired in his second thoughts than in his first. Such a nugget is not likely to be found very often, but to have lighted on even one of this size and quality must hearten any literary goldminer to seek for others.

This series has been projected in the belief that what remains to be done is far more important than the little which has so far been accomplished. It is possible to distinguish already at least four different varieties of Shakespeare texts, each with its own special problems:

(i) the four piracies, *Romeo and Juliet* (1597), *Henry V* (1600), *The Merry Wives of Windsor* (1602), *Hamlet* (1603), besides that of *Pericles* (1609) about which, to be frank, we at present have made no special research;

(ii) the texts of Shakespeare's journeyman's days, notably those of *Henry VI* (all three parts) and *Richard III*, where he was working in collaboration with others, or revising their work, so that we are dealing with other problems besides those of his making;

(iii) the texts for which we have both a 'good' Quarto and the Folio, and have to ascertain their relations;

(iv) the texts of later plays for which we have only the Folio.

Thanks to the constant kindness of the editor of *The Literary Supplement* of *The Times*, Mr Wilson and I have been able to put in print, at least in outline, a theory as to the four piracies, and I have myself

INTRODUCTION xxvii

dealt, even more sketchily, with the York and Lancaster Plays which form part of group (ii). In articles in *The Athenaeum*, Mr Wilson has written on the literary problems of *Hamlet* as well as in *The Library* on the more strictly bibliographical ones. We hope that volumes of the series will grow out of each of these preliminary handlings. For groups (iii) and (iv), we have at present but scanty materials, but we know already that there are plenty to be found. The printers of the Quartos, the editors of the Folio, have alike been blamed for doing so little to present Shakespeare's plays in a worthy form, for not correcting obvious errors, for not even dividing the texts uniformly into Acts and Scenes. We should rather be thankful that these honest men were content with printing the copies from which they had to work with so little alteration. Where they have asserted themselves they have done real harm which can never be entirely righted. Their refusal to edit their material is always our gain. On almost every page of the Quartos and First Folio there is to be found some clue to the history of the text which the literary editors have either despised as beneath their notice or treated as an error introduced by the printers, without ever asking why or how the printers should have so mishandled straightforward copy, if it was straightforward copy that they had before them. We hope by noting and classifying these clues—stage-directions which should have been re-written, line-arrangements which should have been re-divided, strange spellings which should have been normalized, even misprints which should never have been made—to contribute something to the solution of problems which have already occupied the attention of scholars and even of problems, of no less importance, which as yet have scarcely been raised. By dealing with them in separate booklets we hope to continue to advance safely, step by step, and to use the experience gained from the problems of one group in dealing with those of another. It is all pioneer work and we ask for the indulgence which pioneers may fairly claim and which up to the present we gratefully acknowledge has been most generously extended to us.

ALFRED W. POLLARD.

5 *April*, 1920.

THE REGULATION OF THE BOOK TRADE IN THE SIXTEENTH CENTURY

LEGAL writers on English copyright have not shown much interest in the steps by which the conception of literary property was gradually built up, nor are any data easily accessible for comparing the course of its development in England and foreign countries. The accident by which our first English printer was also an exceptionally prolific literary producer and possessed of considerable influence at Court might well have led to a very early recognition of an author's rights to the fruits of his brain, had there been any competitor possessed of sufficient capital to be a really formidable pirate. In Germany, Italy, and France literary work of a kind for which copyright could now be claimed accounted for only quite a small proportion of the output of the earliest presses. The demand in Germany was mainly for printed editions of the ponderous text books of the previous three centuries. Italy added to these an even greater appetite for the Latin classics. In France, more especially at Lyons, there was a healthy demand for works, both imaginative and didactic, in the vernacular. But Caxton's fertility as a translator can hardly be paralleled in the fifteenth century, and this despite the fact that he came to the task late in life and burdened himself almost simultaneously with the cares of a printing-house. A single book from his press, the *Chronicles of England*, which happens also to contain a long piece of original, or semi-original, writing probably from his pen, was reprinted by both Machlinia and (with additions) by the St Albans printer. His other works may have had a natural protection in the fact that, with so small a market as England then offered, to reprint one of them, with no hope of any help such as Caxton himself received from patrons, might have been but a risky adventure. In any case there was no general piratical attack on Caxton's publications, and thus the one English printer and man of letters who possessed the advantage of powerful friends at Court was never driven into a course of self-defence, which could hardly have failed to be helpful to all other honest men pursuing the same callings.

About the time of Caxton's death we begin to hear, first at Venice, afterwards in other Italian cities, and then, in the course of the next twenty years or so, in all the chief printing centres of Europe, of Privileges, by which on the petition usually of a printer, sometimes of an author or editor, other printers were forbidden to reprint the privileged work for a period of years, mostly ten, but sometimes not more than two. Of course, the prohibition was only effective within the dominion of the issuing authority; but the importation and sale of reprints were also forbidden, and there was a fine for every copy contumaciously produced, imported, or sold. Privileges were granted most frequently for works on the production of which it could be shown that a good deal of money had been spent, whether original or not: A striking instance of this is the privilege granted

IN THE SIXTEENTH CENTURY 3

by the Emperor for the Greek Testament edited by Erasmus and printed by Froben, a privilege which probably caused the otherwise unaccountable delay in publishing the New Testament in the Complutensian Polyglot for some years after it was printed, and this despite the fact that the Polyglot was produced by a Cardinal and approved by the Pope.

Grants of Privileges seem to entitle us to argue on the one hand that there was some practical danger of piracy, and on the other that there was no legal recognition of literary rights by appeal to which piracy could be defeated. The first appearance known to me of a privilege for an English printed book is on the Latin sermon preached by Richard Pace at St Paul's Cathedral on the Peace between England and France. This was printed by Pynson, who finished it on 13th November, 1518, and stated at the end of the colophon that it was issued 'cum priuilegio à rege indulto ne quis hanc orationem intra biennium in regno Angliæ imprimat aut alibi impressam et importatam in eodem regno Angliæ vendat.' For a sermon preached on a special occasion a privilege for two years was probably as good as one in perpetuity. In those attached to Horman's *Vulgaria* of 1519, and several later works from Pynson's press, no term is mentioned, the phrases used being simply 'cum priuilegio regis Henrici,' or 'cum priuilegio a rege indulto,' or in English, 'with priuilege to him granted by our souerayne lorde the king.'

The security bestowed on a book by the grant of a privilege was entirely reasonable, but the method of granting it was entirely bad. Every notice on a book that it was protected against piracy carried with it an implication that a book which possessed no

4 REGULATION OF THE BOOK TRADE

privilege might be pirated with impunity. If Caxton had been inspired to appeal to a Court of Equity when Machlinia reprinted the *Chronicles of England*, on the principle that for every wrong there is a remedy he might have won his case, or rather, if we allow for the law's delays in Tudor times, it might have been decided in his favour many years after he and Machlinia were both dead and their estates had been swallowed up by the costs of the litigation. It is not certain that he would have won it, because before printing made it possible to put several hundred copies of a book on the market at the same time, an author's 'rights' had no pecuniary value apart from the gifts which he might receive in return for presentation copies. The gifts, being gifts, might very probably have been ignored by the Courts as uncertain and indeterminate, while the profits from a printed edition might have been looked on askance as something too new to be recognized. Legal decisions in the second half of the eighteenth century established the doctrine that authors had always possessed a natural right to the fruits of their labour, but accompanied this declaration with the corollary that as soon as Parliament legislated on the subject by the Copyright Act passed in 1709, the limited statutory rights then conferred took the place of the natural rights, and left them unenforceable[1]. It might well have been

---

[1] This was finally laid down by the House of Lords in the case of *Millar* v. *Taylor* in 1774. That the author had an exclusive right of first printing his own work was decided by the opinions of eight judges to one, two other judges so qualifying their agreement as to make it worthless. The exclusive right of reprinting was decided by seven judges to four, the same majority declaring that the right was in perpetuity. That, on the other hand, the right was 'impeached,

IN THE SIXTEENTH CENTURY 5

argued, that the Privileges granted to particular books from 1518 onwards had the same effect.

It may naturally occur to us to ask by what power an English king, without consulting Parliament, could interfere by the advice of his Council, with such haphazard and essentially destructive benevolence, with literary property. A full answer to this question would take us far beyond the widest limits of bibliography. A practical view of the matter is that what a King of France or an Emperor could do a Tudor King of England would naturally assume that he could do also. In 1518, moreover, Luther had already started on his career as a Reformer, and this soon rendered almost inevitable the claim, which was gradually made all over Europe, that everything which concerned Printing must necessarily be under Government control. In a proclamation, probably issued early in 1529 (Pynson's bill for printing it was passed for payment on 6th March), we find a list of prohibited books. Another appeared in June, 1530; another on 1st January, 1536. On 16th November, 1538, there came yet another proclamation which, after a preamble beginning: 'The Kynges moste royall maiestie beinge enfourmed, that sondry contentious and sinyster opinyone[s], haue by wronge teachynge and naughtye printed bokes, encreaced and growen within this his realme of Englande,' forbids the importation, sale, or publication, 'without his

---

restrained or taken away by the statute of 8 Anne' (the Act of 1709) and the author precluded from any remedy except on the foundation of that statute was decided in two sets of judgments by six judges to five. See the admirable account of the case in Mr Augustine Birrell's *Seven Lectures on the Law and History of Copyright in Books* (Cassell and Co., 1899), especially pp. 124 *sqq.*

6 REGULATION OF THE BOOK TRADE

maiesties speciall licence,' of any English books printed abroad, and then proceeds:

Item that no persone or persons in this realme, shall from hensforth print any boke in the englyshe tonge, onles vpon examination made by some of his gracis priuie counsayle, or other suche as his highnes shall appoynte, they shall haue lycence so to do, and yet so hauynge, not to put these wordes *Cum priuilegio regali*, without addyng *ad imprimendum solum*, and that the hole copie, or els at the least theffect of his licence and priuilege be therwith printed, and playnely declared and expressed in the Englyshe tonge vnderneth them.

After this come special regulations as to printing the Scriptures, which need not here be rehearsed. The important point for us is that here we have the first of several enactments which forbade the printing of any book in English except after it had been examined by *some* (which implies two or more) of the Privy Council, 'or other suche as his highnes shall appoynte.'

Incidentally we may note that while a licence to print and a privilege carrying with it protection against piratical competition ought to have been kept clearly distinct, the one word 'priuilegium' seems to have been used as a Latin equivalent for both, the reason being, I believe, that King Henry VIII, who re-wrote this clause with his own hand, was not in the least concerned at the moment with the commercial effect of the proclamation, but only with maintaining his own right of censorship. Every book, as I understand the proclamation, required a licence; but this licence was not to be paraded by the use of the words 'Cum priuilegio regali,' without these words being limited and restricted by the addition

IN THE SIXTEENTH CENTURY 7

'ad imprimendum solum.' These must therefore be construed 'only for printing,' i.e. they did not, unless this was expressly stated, confer the royal approbation and they did not in themselves prohibit piracy, though the 'whole copy' or 'effect' of the privilege, when it is printed as the Proclamation directs, probably always contains this prohibition. There is sufficient evidence that by the reign of Elizabeth the words 'ad imprimendum solum' had come to be generally interpreted as equivalent to 'for sole, or exclusive, printing.' Whether or no they can legitimately bear this meaning in Tudor Latin, it seems quite clear from this Proclamation that this is not the meaning they were originally intended to bear.

On 8th July, 1546, there was issued another proclamation 'to auoide and abolish suche englishe bookes as conteine pernicious and detestable errours and heresies' which, while it suggests, as we can gather from other evidence, that the stringent regulations of its predecessor had been inoperative, is itself, as far as it relates to printing, framed on more reasonable lines. The clause concerning this reads:

> Moreouer the kynges maiesty strayghtly chargeth and commaundeth, vpon the peine aforesayde [i.e. imprisonment and fine], that from henceforth no printer do print any maner of englishe boke, balet or playe, but he put in his name to the same, with the name of thautour, and daye of the printe, and shall presente the fyrst copye to the mayre of the towne where he dwelleth, and not to suffer any of the copies to go out of his handes within two dayes next following.

Mayors being usually busy persons, with their own trades or crafts to attend to, it was distinctly hard on them to be saddled with the task of reading any book

8 REGULATION OF THE BOOK TRADE

printed in their town within eight and forty hours of the deposit of a copy. But as far as the printer was concerned, nothing could be more reasonable, and bibliographers and librarians might have blessed Henry VIII if he could have ensured that 'every englishe boke, balet, or playe' should bear the name of the author, the name of the printer, and the day on which it was completed. Unfortunately the proclamation came towards the very close of Henry VIII's reign and had very little effect.

Edward VI took up the subject, at the end of a querulous proclamation of 28th April, 1551, on the worst possible lines.

> And forbicause diuers Printers, Bokeselers, and Plaiers of Enterludes, without consideracion or regarde to the quiet of the realme, do print, sel, and play whatsoeuer any light and phantastical hed listeth to inuent and deuise, whereby many inconueniences hath, and dayly doth arise and follow, amonge the kinges maiesties louyng and faithful subiectes: His highnes therfore straightly chargeth and commaundeth that from hencefurth, no printer or other person do print nor sel, within this Realme or any other his maiestis dominions, any matter in thenglish tong, nor they nor any other person, do sel, or otherwise dispose abrode any matter, printed in any forreyn dominion in thenglishe tongue, onles thesame be firste allowed by his maiestie, or his priuie counsayl in writing signed with his maiesties most gratious hand or the handes of sixe of his sayd priuie counsayl, vpon payne of Imprisonment, without bayle or mayneprice, and further fine at his maiesties pleasor.

In the same way Queen Mary, in a proclamation of 18th August, 1553, soon after she came to the throne, after condemning the 'pryntynge of false fonde bookes,

IN THE SIXTEENTH CENTURY 9

ballettes, rymes, and other lewde treatises in the englyshe tonge, concernynge doctryne in matters now in question and controuersye, touchynge the hyghe poyntes and misteries of christen religion, whiche bokes, ballettes, rymes and treatises are chiefly by the Prynters and Stacioners sette out to sale to her graces subiectes, of an euyll zeale, for lucre and couetous of vyle gayne,' charged and commanded her subjects, not 'to prynte any bookes, matter, ballet, ryme, interlude, processe or treatyse nor to playe any interlude, except they haue her graces speciall licence in writynge for the same, vpon payne to incurre her highnesse indignation and displeasure.'

Probably, though it is not so stated, this 'speciall licence in writynge' was only required for books dealing with religious controversies. In two subsequent proclamations, of 13th June, 1555, and 6th June, 1558, heretical books were again condemned the second proclamation going so far as to declare that any one 'founde to haue any of the sayde wycked and seditious bokes...shall be reputed and taken for a rebell, and shall without delay be executed for that offence accordyng to thordre of marshall lawe.'

The importance of Mary's reign for our purpose lies not in these proclamations, but in the grant of a Charter to the Stationers' Company, which speedily raised it to great importance. But for understanding the motives which dictated the grant of a Charter, the ferocious threat which we have just quoted is not without relevance. In normal times a Tudor monarch, desiring to increase his control over any trade, would have wrapped up his real purpose with professions of love and care for his subjects, or complimentary

10 REGULATION OF THE BOOK TRADE

remarks on the efficiency of English craftsmen, such as form the preamble of the Act of 1534, restricting, for ecclesiastical and political reasons, the importation of books from abroad. Hence, when we find the whole charter dominated by the idea of suppressing prohibited books, we might suspect that the initiative had come from the Stationers, who put forward the need for such an absolute control of the trade in order to persuade Philip and Mary to give them a monopoly. Dr Arber, though he did not advance this particular argument, was quite sure that the initiative came from the Stationers. Thus he wrote (*Transcript*, vol. 1. xxvi.):

The origin and occasion of the Company of Stationers has been much misunderstood. It has been usually thought that King Philip and Queen Mary grouped the hitherto scattered Printers and Stationers into one Company and in London in order to exercise a more effectual control over all English printed books: whereas it was the printing and publishing trade which had long been organized as a City Craft that sought the royal incorporation and the civic livery for its own greater honour and importance.

Dr Arber based this view on a statement by Christopher Barker in 1582, in which he makes him say that 'the Company *procured* a charter,' and italicizes the word 'procured.' But the statement, as he quotes it on his next page, does not use the word 'procured.' What Barker said is: 'Moreover the printer and Stacioners of the same *obteined* a ch[art]re for a Corporacõn by reason of the disorder in pryntynge did so greatlie encrease, to the ende we might restrayne many euilles which would haue happened in the saide profession.' Dr Arber contended that the disorders and evils were trade dis-

IN THE SIXTEENTH CENTURY

orders and trade evils, but when Barker goes on to speak of avoiding 'the disordered behauiour of prynters and suche troubles that might grow by printing,' etc., we must surely interpret his language by the wording of the Charter itself, which says nothing about benefiting the trade, but bases the whole case for a charter on the need for dealing with prohibited books. Under normal circumstances, as we have said, the Charter might be interpreted by inversion. But Philip and Mary were already bitterly angry, and the fact that less than a year later they are found threatening to execute by martial law anyone possessing a heretical book explains the absence of any smooth phrases in the Charter of 1557. When they said that they were actuated by a desire to suppress (what they considered) bad books, they told the truth, and there is no need to go behind their own statement.

That the initiative in the grant of a Charter came from the Crown is made more probable by the contemporary enactments in Spain. According to Mr Barwick ('Laws regulating Printing in Spain,' *Bibliographical Society's Transactions*, iv. 48):

In 1554...an order was issued vesting the licensing power in the Royal Council alone. In 1558 Philip II forbad the sale of imported books before they were licensed, under penalty of death and confiscation of property. This law was made retrospective and those already in stock were to be sent to the Council for approval, under penalty of transportation and confiscation. In this law is first introduced the system, that in the copy submitted to the Council, each page should be signed by one of its notaries, and the errata be entered at the end, the type was then corrected, and the printer was bound to return the signed

12 REGULATION OF THE BOOK TRADE

copy with one or two copies of the impression, and it was likewise ordered that the names of the author, printer and place of printing should be placed in the book. The penalty for any contravention was banishment and confiscation.

Dr Arber would hardly have maintained that *this* enactment was prompted by love of the Spanish Stationers, and although Philip was not in England at the time that the Charter was granted to their English brethren, it seems probable that the underlying motive was the same in each case.

The Charter begins with a preamble as to the need of suppressing objectionable books, recites the names of the Master, Wardens, and Members of the Company, invests the Company with all the usual powers of a Corporation, such as suing in common, etc., prohibits any printing by anyone not a member of the Company, and gives to the Master and Wardens power of imprisonment, a right of search, etc. We shall have to say more about the Company later on. For the moment all that we are concerned with is the ease with which henceforth the Crown could control the whole printing trade. Henceforth every printer was known and under strict regulation, and a body of expert detectives was enlisted in the Government service, able to make a shrewd guess as to whence the type in which any pamphlet or bill was printed had been obtained, and with their own personal interest in helping to suppress any illicit work.

When Elizabeth, the year after she came to the throne, issued the 'Injunctions' of 1559, the Stationers' Company was still in its early days, and although reference is made to the Company in the fifty-first Injunction, which deals with books and printing, the attitude taken up is still that of the earlier Proclamations. The Injunction reads:

51. Item, because there is a great abuse in the Printers of bookes, which for couetousness cheefely, regard not what they print, so that they may haue gaine, whereby ariseth great disorder by publication of vnfruitefull, vaine, and infamous bookes and papers, the Queenes maiestie straitlye chargeth and commaundeth, that no manner of person shall print any manner of booke or paper, of what sort, nature or in what language soeuer it be, excepte the same bee firste licensed by her Maiestie, by expresse wordes in writing, or by six of her priuie counsel: or be perused and licensed by the Archbishops of Canterburie and Yorke, the Bishop of London, the Chauncelors of both Vniuersities, the Bishop being Ordinarye and the Archdeacon also of the place, where any such shal be printed or by two of them, wherof the Ordinarie of the place to be alwayes one. And that the names of such as shall allowe the same to bee added in the end of euery such worke, for a testimonie of the alowance thereof. And because many pamphelets, playes and ballads, bee oftentimes printed, wherein regard woulde bee had, that nothing therein should be either heretical, seditious, or vnseemely for Christian eares: her Maiestie likewise commaundeth, that no maner of person shall enterprise to print any such excepte the same bee to him licensed by suche her Maiesties Commissioners, or three of them, as be appointed in the Cittie of London, to heare and determine diuers causes Ecclesiasticall, tending to the execution of certain statutes, made the last Parliament for vniformitie of order in Religion. And if any shall sell or vtter any maner of bookes or papers, being not licensed, as is abouesayde: that the same partie shalbe punished by order of the saide Commissioners, as to the qualitie of the fault shalbe thought meete. And touching all other bookes of matters of religion, or pollicie, or gouernance, that hath bene printed eyther on this side

the Seas, or on the other side, because the diuersitie of them is great, and that there nedeth good consideration to be had of the particularities thereof, her Maiestie referreth the prohibition or permission thereof, to the order whiche her sayde Commissioners within the Cittie of London shall take and notifie. According to the whiche, her Maiestie straitly commaundeth all maner her subiectes, and specially the Wardens and company of Stationers to be obedient.

Prouided that these orders doe not extende to any prophane [i.e. classical] aucthours, and works in any language that hath ben heretofore commonly receiued or allowed in any of the vniuersities or schooles, but the same may be printed and vsed as by good order they were accustomed.

(B.M. C. 37. e. 53.)

It seems not improbable that whoever drafted this Injunction was much better acquainted with Edward VI's Proclamation of 28th April, 1551, which has a similar mention of six Privy Councillors, or Mary's of 18th August, 1553, which in like manner vituperates Printers and Stationers as being 'of an euyll zeale for lucre and couetous of vyle gayne,' than with the Charter recently granted to the Stationers. It is certainly noteworthy that by the inclusion among the licensing authorities of 'the Bishop being Ordinarie and the Archdeacon also of the place, where any such shal be printed, or by two of them, whereof the Ordinarie of the place to be alwayes one,' the writer of the Injunction clearly contemplated the existence of provincial presses, such as had come into being in the reign of Edward VI at Ipswich, Worcester, and Canterbury, whereas by the Charter granted to the London stationers provincial printing had been absolutely suppressed.

A still stronger argument that the draftsman of the fifty-first Injunction was ignorant that a much

IN THE SIXTEENTH CENTURY 15

better way of dealing with the book-trade had already been found may seem to be the fact that it was almost universally disregarded. This, however, seems to have been the fate of the similar provisions in the various proclamations of the three previous reigns, and we shall make a great mistake if we imagine that because they were thus disregarded they were therefore inoperative. Bread has to be won and the day's work got through despite of risks, and just as French and Belgian peasants have dug their potatoes and collected their handful of sticks with shells falling on the other end of the field, so the Tudor printers and publishers took their risks, and seldom troubled to comply with impossible regulations, such as that requiring the signatures of six privy councillors to authorise the publication of a ballad. But the shells which an old woman disregards prove the existence of guns which may prevent the advance of an army, and throughout the reign of Elizabeth the control of the book trade by the ministers of the Crown was as nearly as possible complete.

In 1566 an Order in Council repeated some of the provisions of the Injunction of 1559, and took power to call upon any printer to find security for his good behaviour. In 1572 the usefulness of the Stationers' Company was proved by the success with which it hunted down the secret Puritan press which printed Cartwright's *Admonition to the Parliament*, and it is noteworthy that throughout the rest of the reign of Elizabeth we hear of only two other secret presses of any importance, that in the Jesuit interest, which printed Campion's *Rationes decem* in 1581, and the famous Marprelate Press, which defied the Government with some success in 1588–9. On the other hand, Elizabeth and her advisers made serious trouble for themselves by continuing the bad practice of granting privileges not merely for individual books, but for whole classes of books. As early as 1544, possibly to console them for dropping money over their Bibles, Grafton and Whitchurch had been granted such a privilege for printing service books. In 1552 Tottell was granted a similar privilege for law books, and in that and the following year John Day had received the valuable monopoly of the *Catechism in English* and *ABC*. In Elizabeth's reign Thomas Marshe was granted exclusive rights in printing Latin books for use in schools, and Richard Watkins in English almanacs. As long as Archbishop Parker lived, the printing of English Bibles was kept in the hands of Richard Jugge (who, perhaps by the Archbishop's orders, made scanty use of it), while, with equal suavity and firmness, Parker rendered wholly inoperative the privileges granted to Bodley and his friends for printing the Geneva version. But the breath was hardly out of Parker's body when trouble began. For the first time we hear of a formal compliance with the Injunctions of 1559, and seven privy councillors (one more than was needed) licensed Christopher Barker, a protégé of Sir Francis Walsingham's, to print the Geneva Bible and New Testament. In 1577, moreover, after a pecuniary arrangement for the benefit of Sir Thomas Wilkes, a Privy Councillor of some importance, Barker was appointed Printer to the Queen, and received a monopoly for printing Bibles, service-books, statutes, proclamations, and all books ordered to be printed by the Queen or Parliament.

The strife which followed the issue of this patent

IN THE SIXTEENTH CENTURY 17

lasted very nearly as long as the Trojan War, and the details of it are beside our purpose. It began with quarrels between Barker and the earlier patentees, some of whose privileges, notably those of Tottell for law printing, the new patent infringed. It speedily led to a much more serious struggle between the privileged and non-privileged printers, in which it is clear that popular sympathy was strongly on the side of the non-privileged, or the extraordinary boldness with which their leaders, Roger Ward and John Wolfe, defied Queen and Council, would have led to a very different result. The Council insisted on the Queen's right to grant privileges being maintained, and maintained it was, though the Commissioners appointed to enquire into the trouble had mildly deprecated the use made of it. In other respects the malcontents secured notable gains. John Wolfe was bought off by being appointed City Printer. The privileged printers placed the right of reprinting many of their books in the hands of the Stationers' Company, to be used to find work for the poorer printers. The Company itself passed an ordinance restricting the number of copies of which an edition might consist, so as to secure more work for compositors, and also restricted the number of apprentices and forbade their employment on work which a journeyman of good character was ready to perform. Finally, the notorious 'Newe Decrees of the Starre Chamber for order in Printing' of 23rd June, 1586, though prejudice against the Star Chamber has caused them to be generally regarded as merely repressive, were assuredly at least partly inspired by an honest desire to find a remedy for these economic troubles, which were felt to be dangerous.

18 REGULATION OF THE BOOK TRADE

The key to the situation is supplied by the fact that the test-case of the struggle was the claim that anyone who pleased should be allowed to print the *A B C* with the *Little Catechism*, a book for which there was a continual demand, which presented no difficulties, literary or typographical, for which, indeed, the poorest printing would suffice, and no author nor editor had to be paid. The total number of men engaged in the printing trade at this time was less than two hundred, but small as this number may seem, it was more than there was work for. The larger printers laid stress, and we must take due note of it, on the fact that unless they were secured against piracy, they could not afford to pay 'a learned man' to write or edit a book. The learned men naturally took their wares to the larger firms, who could both print better and pay better, and where, as by now was mostly the case, a publisher intervened, he too would naturally take his books to the larger printers, who printed better, and could employ him to publish the books over which they, as printers, possessed rights. The remedy which the Star Chamber proposed, a reduction in the number of printing-presses, in so far as it was carried out, must have tended to put more work into the hands of any printer who possessed a press. An unused press was equally obnoxious to the wealthier members of the Stationers' Company and the Government, for sooner or later it might be used to print either the *A B C* or a more or less treasonable pamphlet. Even after the 'Newe Decrees' of the Star Chamber a printer with a press and a handful of type, eager to make a bit of bread by using them, was a potential pirate.

Having said something as to the part played by

IN THE SIXTEENTH CENTURY

the Privy Council in regulating the Printing trade, and as to the genesis of Pirates, a little must be added about the Stationers' Company, which thus far we have considered only as the instrument of the Privy Council for the suppression of inconvenient literature. The Company claims to have been formed, out of two earlier ones, in 1404. At what date printers were first admitted to it is still doubtful. Caxton was a Mercer, and had no reason to become a Stationer, nor can we imagine that the Stationers would have welcomed very cordially the introducer of so formidable an innovation as the new art of printing. As all, or nearly all, his contemporaries and immediate successors, Lettou, Machlinia, Wynkyn de Worde, Pynson and Faques, possibly also Julian Notary, were foreigners, whatever prejudice existed would not lightly die out. Possibly Peter Actors, though a native of Savoy, was admitted to the Company in virtue of his appointment as Stationer to the King, and when William Faques succeeded Actors, though he called himself Printer, not Stationer, to the King, the Stationers may have accepted him also. Certainly Pynson, who succeeded Faques as royal printer, seems to have been a member of the Company, since in his will he directs that John Snowe and Richard Withers 'shall serve their yeares at the assignment of my executrix. And at thende of their said yeres my said executrix to make them free of my craft.' Wynkyn de Worde's will explicitly speaks of his executor, John Bedill (or Byddell), as 'citizen & stacioner of London,' and of the three overseers of the will, Henry Pepwell, John Gough and Robert Copland, as 'Stacioners.' Whether De Worde himself was a Stationer is less certain. The freedom with which he reprinted some

20 REGULATION OF THE BOOK TRADE

of Pynson's books would have been reprehensible in a brother of the same company.

Printers are to us so much more interesting than Stationers that we naturally give them precedence, but it is probable that as a class the Stationers were for many years the wealthier and more influential. It is certainly noteworthy that, according to Mr Duff's extracts from the Lay Subsidy Rolls of 1523–4 (*The Library*, 2nd Series, IX. 257 *sq.*) one Stationer, John Taverner, was assessed at £307 as against De Worde's £201 11*s.* 1*d.*, and another, Richard Nele (who was transferred to the Ironmongers in 1525) at £100 as against Pynson's £60. Thus, even in the first half of the sixteenth century, there is no reason to think that the Stationers would in any way have courted the Printers, and on the other hand members of other companies, for instance, Grafton who was a Grocer, Whitchurch who was a Haberdasher, and John Day who is said, until 1550 or thereabouts, to have been a Stringer, seem to have been able to exercise the craft of Printing without molestation from the Stationers. But be this as it may, at the time that the Company was granted its Charter almost all the practising printers had become members of it. Some of these may have rallied to it only in anticipation of that event; but on the other hand, throughout the 'forties in the lessened encroachment on other men's 'copies' and in the beginning of joint-publication, as in the case of the *Chaucer* of [1545] in which four firms took part, we may perhaps trace the development of what may be called 'Company' manners.

It seems clear that, although neither the injunctions of 1559 nor the Order in Council of 1566 authorized such a course, the Stationers' Company from the outset, and for many years afterwards, acted as a licensing authority. The Company's years ran from July to July, and under the first of them (1557–8), after it received a Charter, we find a rubric (Arber, i. 74): 'The Entrynge of all such Copyes as be lycensed to be printed by the Master and Wardyns of the mystery of stacioners as foloweth.' In the next year (1558–9), which included the accession of Elizabeth, its ability and willingness to exercise authority is shown by the entries under another rubric: 'fynes for defautes for Pryntynge withoute lycense.' The printer of an unlicensed ballad was only fined fourpence, and in the case of an unlicensed book twelvepence, but where the book was of a kind for which special authority would have been expected the fines are much heavier, no less a person than John Day being fined five shillings (equivalent in 1913 to nearly £2 and to about double that now) 'for prynting of a boke without lycense called an Excelent treates made by Nosterdamus,' and Richard Adams the same sum for printing 'the Regester of all them that were burned,' a very controversial topic in the early days of the new reign. An even heavier punishment was inflicted on Richard Lant who had printed without licence an *Epitaph of Queen Mary*, for of him it is recorded that he 'was sent to warde,' i.e. to the Company's private prison. As a typical entry of this period, in the case of an obviously harmless book, we may cite one for 1559:

Recevyd of John daye for his lycense for the pryntynge of the governaunce of vertue the vj of august iiij^d.

As an example of a specially authorized entry we

may take this of the year 1570–71, just before a break in the Company's records:

> Recevyd of Rychard Jones for his lycense for ye pryntinge of morral phelosiphe by [i.e. authorised by] my lord of London.

Save that 'Lycenced to' was frequently substituted for 'Recevyd for his lycense for the printing of,' this form continued in use till 1588, and, in face of it, we must admit that the Company acted as a licensing authority for harmless books. According, however, to a note as to the former practice of licensing books made in 1636 by Sir John Lambe, on 30th June, 1588, 'the Archbishop gave power to Doctor Cosin, Doctor Stallard, Doctor Wood, master Hartwell, master Gravett, Master Crowley, master Cotton and master Hutchinson, or any one of them to license books to be printed: Or any 2 of these following master Judson, master Trippe, master Cole and master Dickens[1].' The appointment of a body of accessible licensers clearly superseded the informal licensing power which the Stationers themselves had

---

[1] Arber, iii. 690. The note of Sir J. Lambe proceeds: 'From 19º Elizabethe till the Starrechamber Decree 28º Elizabethe, many were licensed by the master and Wardens, some few by the master Alone, and some by the Archbishop and more by the Bishop of London. The like was in the former parte of the Quene Elizabeths time. They were made a corporation but by P. and M. Master Kingston, the now master, sayth that before the Decree the master and wardens licensed all, and that when they had any Divinity booke of muche importance they would take the advise of some 2 or 3 ministers of this towne.' Lambe's taking the date '19º Elizabethe' as a starting point suggests that he was writing after glancing through the Stationers' Registers, and that the gap in these from 1571 to 1576 was already there. Neither his note nor Felix Kingston's assertion has any independent authority, but taken together they give substantially the same account as that offered above.

IN THE SIXTEENTH CENTURY 23

previously exercised. Henceforth, though variants occur, the form of an entry on 1st July, 1588:

> Thomas Orwin. Entred to him for his copie, A booke intitled the complaint of tyme Alowed vnder Doctor Stallers hand as profitable to be printed   vj^d.

(omitting the 'as profitable to be printed') became increasingly common, until gradually it ousted all others. After a time the Wardens to some extent recovered their old position as informal licensers, but the use of the form, 'Entred for his copy,' kept the two points involved in the entry (i) a record of permission to print, and (ii) a promise of protection from piracy, much better distinguished than in the older entries.

If we take the two points just mentioned to represent the advance made in the economic position of the English book trade during the sixteenth century, this will at first sight seem very small, and smaller still if we look at it from the standpoint of an author. Until the doctrines of Luther began to spread to England, no permission to print was needed. Amid the religious and political upheaval which resulted from the new teaching the book trade suffered heavily, and doubtless its members congratulated themselves in the year of the Armada on the comparative ease with which a licence could be procured for works which aroused no religious or political objection. The protection from piracy, though unless secured by a royal privilege it had no legal force, but rested solely on the private ordinances of the Stationers' Company, was a real and obvious gain. Moreover, although the ordinances of the Stationers' Company took no account whatever of the rights of authors, it was a gain to these as well as to printers and publishers. Next to being able to secure perpetual copyright in his writings for himself, the best thing that could happen to an author was to be able to sell his books to someone else who could do so. The copyright which the Stationers' Company conferred on the publisher who entered a book on its register, by increasing his prospect of profit made it possible to increase also the remuneration of the author, nor was there such a total absence of competition between rival publishers as to oblige an author to accept whatever he was offered. Literary payments, being a new thing, could not be put on a reasonable footing all at once. By Milton's day, though no change in the legal position had occurred, an author could secure by contract a promise of further payments for later editions. The Elizabethan custom transferred to the publisher the entire property in a book for a single payment, which the possibility of future editions would and could only slightly affect. This was the publisher's gain and the author's loss, but for books of which only a single edition could be sold, there seems no reason to believe that the Elizabethan author obtained worse terms than he would at the present day. The worst payment which we hear of is the twenty-six copies of his book handed over to an obscure writer named Richard Robinson instead of cash; the best, the £40 in money, with maintenance for himself, two servants, and their horses during nine months, which Dr Fulke received from George Bishop for his *Confutation of the Rhemish Testament*. £2 is said to have been the market-price for a popular pamphlet, though Greene or Nash may have obtained double this. Even the doubled sum may seem very little. But parsons and

IN THE SIXTEENTH CENTURY 25

schoolmasters, even fellows of colleges, were apparently considered lucky in Elizabeth's reign if they earned more than £20 a year. These all pursued old established methods of earning a living. It is no matter for wonder if those who tried a newer path found it even stonier. Our only point is that, whether the payments were little or large, in cash, in board and lodging, or in books, the payment of authors had definitely become a trade custom by the end of the sixteenth century. We shall consider in another lecture how far these payments were made precarious by publishers obtaining security for themselves, 'notwithstanding their first Coppies were purloyned from the true owner or imprinted without his leave.' That they did this, is the accusation brought against the booksellers in the *Schollers Purgatory* by George Wither, whose personal grievance was his failure to enforce an iniquitous grant he had obtained from James I, by which no one was to be able to buy a copy of *The Psalms in Metre* without also buying Wither's *Hymns*. The grievance makes Wither a bad witness, but his charge has often been repeated, and we shall have to see what substance there is in it, more especially as regards the plays with which we are mainly concerned.

AUTHORS, PLAYERS, AND PIRATES IN SHAKESPEARE'S DAY

IN writing on the Regulation of the Book Trade in the Sixteenth Century I claimed that the informal copyright which the Stationers' Company was able to secure to its members in the case of any book duly entered on its register, though it seems to us a poor substitute for a legal copyright vested in the author himself, distinctly increased the market value of the literary wares which an author might have to sell. The publisher, when he was protected from piracy, could afford to pay more than when he was not, and authorship became possible as a profession as soon as printers began to respect each others' rights. That the money received from booksellers was miserably small resulted not so much from their rapacity as from the smallness and poverty of the reading public. Moreover, whether little or much, it was a new income. Before the invention of printing an author was entirely dependent upon patronage for his literary rewards. It took three centuries wholly to supersede patronage, and in Shakespeare's day only about a third of the road had been travelled. The starveling author, Richard Robinson, whose account of his winnings Dr McKerrow unearthed some years ago, sold twenty-five of the twenty-six copies which his publisher gave him instead of cash, as a rule at a shilling apiece. Only once did he obtain as much as forty shillings for the lot. It was on the reward he obtained for the twenty-sixth copy, the one presented to the patron selected as dedicatee, that the success or failure of a book depended. Once the poor wretch flew too high, and making the Queen herself his victim, came off empty-handed. Once, on the other hand, he obtained no less than £3, and proudly records that for a whole year thereafter he was no burden to his friends. Next best to this came a reward of thirty shillings from Sir Henry Sidney, supplemented by another ten from his son Philip. The gifts of other dedicatees were sometimes not more than a few shillings.

The system of patronage, of which Richard Robinson was a product, retarded the development of authorship as a profession in two ways: directly, by encouraging publishers to give less money on the plea that the patron would make it up; indirectly, by so lowering the status of authors who tried to live by their pens that no one with any pretension to rank or fashion could take money for his writings. To escape any imputation of doing so, fashionable authors avoided print altogether, and circulated their writings among their friends in manuscript. It was this practice which encouraged piracy more than anything else. The relatives of Sir Philip Sidney could not have pleaded that his estate was defrauded by his *Apology for Poetry*, or his *Astrophel*, or *Arcadia*, being printed by a publisher who had got hold of one of the manuscript copies. Under no circumstances would Philip Sidney, who, poor as he was, was a liberal patron of letters, have put himself on a level with those he patronized by taking money from a publisher. His relatives could only say that they objected, and in an ordinary court of law it is hard to see how they could have obtained any redress. For here custom was all against them. If a medieval author circulated a book in manuscript he could not prevent other copies being made from it, though there may well have been cases in which it would have been thought shabby in an owner to permit this. Even the Elizabethan man of fashion who wrote out his poems for his friends had no remedy against copying in manuscript, and except on the ground of pecuniary damage, which a man of any distinction was debarred from pleading, it is hard to see how an Elizabethan judge could have ruled that to copy in manuscript was permissible, but to copy in print, not.

Just because all matters connected with printing were under the almost absolute control of the Privy Council and the Archbishop of Canterbury, the Sidney family defeated the interfering publisher in every case; but the existence of a class of writers who neither did, nor could, take money for their books was none the less a great clog on the development of professional authorship, and introduced possibilities of genuine mistakes. We all know to what shifts Pope was reduced when he wanted the world to see what beautiful letters he was in the habit of writing to his friends, and recognized that literary etiquette, or perhaps we should say 'decent feeling,' forbade him to publish them himself. By devices which soon became obvious, though their full exposure was reserved for literary antiquaries almost of our own day, he procured their publication by the notorious pirate, Edmund Curll, and thus, though with much loss of credit, secured his object. In the sixteenth century any aristocratic author, or any author who wished to be thought equally scrupulous

IN SHAKESPEARE'S DAY

on what was then considered a point of honour, found himself debarred from publishing his poems or other contributions to the fashionable literature of the day by a convention of very much the same kind as Pope, in the case of his private letters, only surmounted by disgraceful intrigues.

The preliminary matter of Barnabe Googe's *Eglogs and Epytaphes*, printed by Thomas Colwell for Raufe Newbery in 1563, shows us one way in which an author's pretty hesitations about committing his poems to print could be surmounted. In 1562, when Googe went on a visit to Spain, he left the manuscript of his verses in the keeping of a friend named Blundeston, who took on himself to send them to be printed, and explained at some length, both in verse and prose, how desire for his friend's fame prompted him to do so. The author's own story is given in his dedication: 'To the ryght worshipfull M. William Louelace, Esquier, Reader of Grayes Inne,' in which he asserts that his sense of the grossness of his style and distrust of 'scornefull and carpynge Correctours' caused him rather to condemn his poems to

continuall darkenes, wherby no Inconuénience could happen: than to endaunger my selfe in gyuynge them to lyght, to the disdaynfull doome of any offended mynde. Notwithstandynge[,] all the dylygence that I coulde vse in the Suppression therof coulde not suffise[,] for I my selfe beyng at that tyme oute of the Realme, lytell fearynge any suche thynge to happen A verye Frende of myne, bearynge as it semed better wyll to my doynges than respectyng the hazarde of my name, commytted them all togyther vnpolyshed to the handes of the Prynter. In whose handes durynge his absence from the Cytie, tyll his returne of late they remayned. At whiche tyme, he declared the matter wholly vnto me: shewynge me that beynge so farre past, & Paper prouyded for the Impression therof: It coulde not withoute greate hynderaunce of the poore Printer be nowe reuoked. His sodayne tale made me at ye fyrst, vtterly amazed, and doubting a great while, what was best to be done: at the lengthe agreying both with Necessytie and his Counsell, I sayde with Martiall *I iam sed poteras tutior esse domi*

and allowed the printer to proceed.

Googe's account of what happened is probably very fairly true. Had he been lying, he would not have confessed that at the time of his return printing had not yet begun, with the implication that by merely compensating Colwell for his loss on reselling the paper or holding it till it could be used on some other book, he could have kept his poems in safe obscurity. It is interesting to note, though we need not lay stress on it, that he assumes that he could have recalled his manuscript, and have left the printer to bear such loss as might result. But it sufficed for him to make consideration for 'the poore Printer' his excuse for publication, and it may suffice for us to point out what a confusing element the existence of busybodies or enthusiasts like Googe's friend Blundeston must have introduced into the book trade.

Blundeston was a real person and a real friend of Googe's, whether he played a friend's part in this transaction or not. A generation later, however, it is hardly surprising that the genuine enthusiasts, of whom we may take him as a type, should be very difficult to distinguish on the one hand from such a shadowy scapegoat as the 'some' whom Wm Percy made responsible for the publication of his *Sonnets to the fairest Coelia* in 1594, and on the other hand from such professional dealers in manuscripts as Thomas Thorpe and William Hall, as to whose doings Sir Sidney Lee has brought together so much useful information in his account of the publication of Shakespeare's *Sonnets*. It will be useful to remember that one of these began his career by procuring a manuscript of Marlowe's (his translation of the first book of Lucan's *Pharsalia*), and the other by getting hold of Robert Southwell's *A Foure-fould Meditation*; and that both Marlowe and Southwell were dead, and the works of one as a reputed atheist and of the other as a notorious Jesuit would be to an unusual extent at the disposal of anyone who had the courage to print them. On the other hand, Thorpe must have obtained Chapman's consent to publishing two of his plays, his *Byron* and *All Fools*, as we find that to all copies of the first and to some of the second Chapman prefixed a dedication. It may be doubted indeed if it can be proved, even in the case of Thorpe or Hall, that they plied their trade without any respect to the pecuniary rights of living professional authors. It is possible, perhaps probable, that Shakespeare's *Sonnets* were published by Thorpe in 1609 without his consent, and that he would have stopped their publication if he could. Into that thorny question we fortunately need not enter. But it is very much to our purpose to note that the *Sonnets* in 1609 had been in existence for some fifteen years, that Meres in his *Palladis Tamia* had commended them in print in 1598, and that yet, with the exception of two printed in *The Passionate Pilgrim* the following year (1599), no printer had been willing or able to appropriate them. They may have been pirated at last, but they escaped for fifteen years.

It may be worth while here to quote from Nashe's dedication of *The Terrors of the Night* to Mistres Elizabeth Carey his assertions as to its popularity in manuscript:

> As touching this short glose or annotation on the foolish Terrors of the Night...A long time since hath it line suppressed by mee: vntill the vrgent importunitie of a kinde frend of mine (to whom I was sundrie waies beholding) wrested a Coppie from me. That Coppie progressed from one scriueners shop to another, & at length grew so common, that it was readie to bee hung out for one of their signes, like a paire of indentures. Wherevppon I thought it as good for mee to reape the frute of my owne labours, as to let some vnskilfull pen-man or Nouerint-maker startch his ruffle & new spade his beard with the benefite he made of them.

Although the booklet was being so repeatedly copied by different scriveners not only did none of them make a second copy and sell it to a printer, but Nashe does not seem even to have considered the possibility of this being done. It is solely the benefit or pay which the 'vnskilfull pen-man' might make by producing manuscript copies that he grudges him. Yet in 1594 a pamphlet by Nashe had probably as high a selling value as any other book of the same length that was being put on the market.

The point we are making is that the appropriation of literary rights without permission or payment which we call piracy, in so far as it can be proved, was largely concerned with the works of dead authors, or of men whose rank would have forbidden them to receive payment for their books. The talk about books being printed without leave is at least sometimes only doubtfully sincere. Men who were known to

IN SHAKESPEARE'S DAY

be making a living from their pens seem to have suffered very little indeed from piracy, even when, as in the case of the book by Nashe just mentioned, they laid themselves easily open to attack.

In this connection we shall do well to remember that there was no change in the law, or in the apparent, though not quite real, exclusion of authors from the benefit of such copyright as the Stationers' Company could secure, for exactly a hundred years after the publication of Shakespeare's *Sonnets*. In 1624, in his *Schollers Purgatory*, George Wither wrote of the Stationers:

Yea, by the lawes and Orders of their Corporation, they can and do setle vpon the particuler members thereof a p[e]rpetuall interest in such Bookes as are Registered by them at their Hall, in their several Names: and are secured in taking the full benefit of those books, better then any Author can be by virtue of the Kings Grant, notwithstanding their first Coppies were purloyned from the true owner, or imprinted without his leave.

In whatever sense this assertion was true at the time when Wither made it, it was true also when Milton was able to make a formal contract securing him a share in the profits of more editions of *Paradise Lost* than were printed during his life, and when Dryden was able to support himself by his pen. Until the first Copyright Act was passed in 1709 there was no change in the law. Whatever else that statute effected (and it might well be contended that it benefited the reading public at the expense of authors) it did not suppress piracy. It was in the year which preceded that Act that Edmund Curll's name is first found on a title-page, and his notorious career extended for some thirty years after it became law.

Yet, though accusations have been levelled at random against this or that Elizabethan printer or publisher, there is not one of them who, as a pirate, can be named in the same breath with Curll.

Curll's piracies did not prevent the position of authors from steadily improving during the eighteenth century. It cannot therefore be argued that the fact that the position of authors undoubtedly improved steadily during the life of Shakespeare proves that there were no piracies in his day. It only proves that they were not on a scale to interfere with the steady development. Piracies there were, and two reasons have here been advanced to explain this much exaggerated but indubitable fact: (i) the presence in London of more printers than there was work for; (ii) the convention which forbade men of rank or fashion from circulating their poems or essays except in manuscript. The first of these sources of trouble was steadily kept in view by the Privy Council, whose interference, usually represented as purely repressive and tyrannical, was in part at least economic and (on the whole) beneficent. The second cause may be presumed to have been largely removed by the succession to the throne, in the person of James I, of 'a prentice in the noble art of poetry' who did not refrain from publication. Even while these two purely transitory causes were in full operation their effect on the English book-trade as a whole was insignificant. We have now to ask whether there were any circumstances peculiar to one branch of the book-trade, that concerned with the publication of plays, which should incline us to believe that it was specially open to attack, and what positive evidence can be found of the attacks having been successful.

IN SHAKESPEARE'S DAY 35

During the middle years of the sixteenth century, when the ecclesiastical future of England was still uncertain, the acting of interludes supporting more or less blatantly either the Roman or the Protestant side seems to have greatly annoyed successive Tudor governments. Elizabeth dealt with the nuisance by an Act declaring all players of interludes to be rogues and vagabonds and liable to the unpleasant penalties provided for these poor folk, unless formed into companies under the protection of a Privy Councillor, who would be answerable for their good behaviour. As the business community became more and more strongly addicted to Puritanism, the rulers of the City of London would gladly have prohibited stage plays altogether. Elizabeth, however, as well as her successors, happened to be very fond of these performances, and on the plea that they must be given opportunities to develop their skill for exhibition at Court, the players were generally protected, although all performances were forbidden during visitations of the plague for fear of infection, and at other times increase of Puritan pressure might restrict the number of them.

The fact that one company of players was under the protection of the Lord High Admiral, and another of the Lord Chamberlain, and that these were two of the most important members of the Privy Council, which, as we have seen, exercised supreme authority over printers and printing, suggests at first that these companies must have had complete protection against interference on the part of pirates. It was the companies with which the pirates would have had to deal, as during the reign of Elizabeth it is certain that the dramatists sold their complete rights to the company which was to act the play, so that it would be the company, not the author, that would be injured by a piracy. That a company with the Lord Chamberlain or the Lord High Admiral as its protector should have submitted to any systematic robbery is in the highest degree unlikely. On the other hand, the hostility of the City and occasional trouble at Court rendered the position of the players always more or less precarious, and to trouble a great lord over a small matter when they might need his help in a much more important one would not have been wise. Hence we need not be surprised if we find a company submitting to occasional loss rather than trouble their protector, as long as the loss does not become too frequent. The market price for a pamphlet towards the end of the sixteenth century seems to have been forty shillings, though the most popular writers obtained more. The selling value of a play must have been much the same as that of a pamphlet. A few when printed went through half a dozen or more editions; many of those we think the best were never reprinted at all, or not in the popular quarto form. To go to the Lord Chamberlain over the loss of a forty-shilling fee for the printing rights in a play would hardly have been good business.

On the other hand, if we are tempted to extend this argument to the point of agreeing with the contention that it could never have been worth while for a company to permit its plays to be printed, we must remember that the total sum paid to an author by the company was itself only small, ranging as a rule from £6 to £10 in the latter years of Elizabeth, though as much as £20 seems occasionally to have

IN SHAKESPEARE'S DAY

been paid, and during the next decade may not have been an unusual fee. To recover from a publisher twenty or even ten per cent. of the original price paid for a play cannot have been a matter of indifference, and although at the outset of a play's run it would probably have been bad policy to allow it to be printed for any fee a publisher could have afforded to pay, there must have come a time when the injury, if any, done by publication would have been more than made good even by a return of only a small fraction of the price paid.

On the view here maintained the players' willingness to permit the publication of any individual play would be decided by the conditions of the moment, while their special power of appealing to the Privy Council was a reserve force which secured them against any general attack, but not from isolated and occasional depredations. As regards the Stationers' Company the players held no specially favoured position. It is even possible that some of the more important members of the Company may have taken the official City view that play-acting was a nuisance which ought to be abolished. But except that if a needy printer were earning his bit of bread by pirating a play, he might be a little less likely to be also pirating the *Grammar and Accidence* or the *Catechism with the A B C*, the magnates of the Stationers' Company had no reason to approve of the multiplying of plays by piracy, while they had the very strongest reasons for not embroiling themselves with the Privy Councillors who were the players' protectors.

The defensive position of the players being such as we have described, what were the possible attacking forces, and what power did they possess? We have seen that owing to the lack of work and the uneven distribution of such work as there was, some minor printer was always likely to be in difficulties, and as we know that these men were ready at such times to set the Stationers' Company at defiance by pirating the *Grammar and Accidence* or the *Catechism*, it is not likely that they would be squeamish about pirating a play. Before a play could be printed, however, the text of it had to be obtained, and after it was printed the booklet had to be sold, and neither of these necessary steps was easy. Thomas Heywood, in a preface written to his *Lucrece* in 1608, speaks of early plays of his[1] having 'accidentally come into the printers hands and therefore so corrupt and mangled (coppied only by the eare) that I haue bin as vnable to know them, as ashamed to chalenge them,' and a quarter of a century later in a Prologue written for the revival of his *If you know not me you know nobody, or the Troubles of Queen Elizabeth*, first published in 1605, asserts that

> Some by Stenography drew
> The plot: put it in print: (scarce one word trew:)

Heywood was writing a quarter of a century after the publication of the plays in question, and in other respects is not a very good witness; but taking his statements as they stand we must note, hardly without

[1] The plays of Heywood which had appeared in print before 1608 were the two parts of his *Edward IV* (1600, F. K. for Humfrey Lownes and John Oxenbridge), the two parts of *If you know not me* (1605, 1606, for N. Butter), *A Woman Killed with Kindness* (1607, Wm. Jaggard, sold by John Hodgets), and *The Fair Maid of the Exchange* (1607, for Henry Rockit).

IN SHAKESPEARE'S DAY 39

surprise, his declaration that the stenographic copy came 'accidentally' into the printer's hands, which excludes deliberate piracy on the part either of printer or shorthand writer. If we must venture a guess as to what happened we may remember that at a slightly later date manuscript copies of some of Beaumont and Fletcher's plays circulated among lovers of the drama, and it is possible that the shorthand copies of some of Heywood's plays were made by a scrivener for this comparatively innocent purpose, and that one of these came 'accidentally' into the printer's hands. Heywood's further statement that this was 'vnknown to me and without any of my direction,' it will also be observed, does not oblige us to believe that the company of players to whom he had sold his play outright were also ignorant of the transaction and unconcerned in it. In any case piracy by stenography can hardly, without incredible carelessness on the part of the owners of theatres, have been allowed to grow into a practice. When once detected it could easily be stopped.

Mr Fleay, when he set himself to explain how *Romeo and Juliet* was pirated, supposed that the text in question was the prompter's copy of an unrevised early version, and proceeds: 'When the revision took place this copy would be thrown aside as worthless; and any dishonest employé of the theatre could sell it to an equally dishonest publisher, who would publish it as the play now acted.' If piracy of plays was practically unknown in 1596 the explanation is bibliographically possible, whatever else may be said against it. But if piracy were at all a common danger can we imagine a prompter throwing aside a complete copy of a play for any dishonest servant to pick up and sell; or, if this might happen once, can we believe it to have happened twice?

Dr Greg has suggested the possibility that the traitor in the case of the *Merry Wives of Windsor* may have been the actor who played the part of the Host, the scenes in which the Host appears being more coherently reproduced than the rest. This is technically a sound hypothesis, and the danger to which it points was more likely to be permanent, or recurrent, than those just considered. The 'hired men' in the Elizabethan theatres were poorly paid, and still more poorly esteemed, and if one of them made up his mind to add to his earnings in this fashion, it might have been some time before detection overtook him. If such a treacherous 'hired man' lighted on a printer such as John Danter when the latter was in his worst straits, there was nothing to prevent the piracy from being completed. Danter could hawk the edition among the booksellers without employing a publisher, and as soon as the copies were off his hands his known poverty would make it useless to take action against him. Unless he entered the book on the Register of the Stationers' Company he could claim no copyright in it, but (as we have said) many plays never reached a second edition, so Danter saved the sixpence registration fee, sacrificed the hope of future profit, and was content with his gains on a single edition. Had he flown at the higher game, he might have found himself cross-examined as to the provenance of his copy, and finally have been fobbed off with a conditional entry, 'provided that he get lawful license for it.' If the impecunious copy-snatcher were a bookseller instead of a printer, he might find himself

IN SHAKESPEARE'S DAY 41

obliged to take this risk as the only means of making a profit at all. This seems to have been the case with John Busby when he entered *The Merry Wives of Windsor*, on 18th January, 1602, and assigned it, at the cost of another sixpence, there and then, to Arthur Johnson. If Arthur Johnson had declared himself unwilling to enter the play himself, or to buy the copy before it had been entered, we should have a pretty explanation why two sixpences were spent instead of one.

John Busby brought off his coup, owing probably to his victims being in an unusually defenceless position, of which he was doubtless aware. But in the twenty years July, 1590, to June, 1610, over 150 plays were duly brought before the Stationers' Company and entered, and, although here and there a pirate may have achieved the maximum success of getting a 'stolne and surreptitious' copy registered as his property, bibliographers may well hesitate to believe that such triumphs were frequent until someone propounds an easier way in which they could be achieved. Incredulity will be heightened when we find that a considerable proportion of these entries come close together, as if the books which they represent had been disposed of in batches. Thus in the two years July, 1591, to July, 1593, only six plays were registered; but in the ten months October, 1593, to July, 1594, no fewer than twenty-eight. In 1595 there were eight entries; in 1596 one; in 1597 two; in 1598 four; in 1599 two. Then in 1600 the number rises to twenty-two, and 1601 produced another eight. 1602 has three; 1603 (a plague year) only one; 1604 six; 1605 eleven; 1606 seven; 1607 as many as seventeen; 1608 a dozen,

42 AUTHORS, PLAYERS, AND PIRATES

or if we take the twelvemonth, 22nd March, 1608, to 10th March, 1609, seventeen again, after which no play was entered for another fifteen months. Surely these variations, from one, two or three entries of plays in a twelvemonth to seventeen, twenty-two or twenty-eight, point to a controlled output, to there being years when the supply was rigorously held up and other years when they were offered to the booksellers in such quantities as could only have been produced by the legitimate owners of them. We cannot imagine twenty-eight piracies having immediately preceded the ten months October, 1593, to July, 1594, but we can easily imagine that the players would have been glad to sell this number of plays about that time, because shortly before this there had been a similar period, from April to 22nd December, 1593, during which the theatres were closed because of the plague, and the companies must have been very hard hit. In like manner, though the coincidence is not quite so strong, the outpouring of plays in 1600 and 1601 may be connected with the Puritan attacks on the players which resulted in an Order in Council on 22nd June of the former year, restricting the number of theatres to two, forbidding any performances in Lent, and allowing only two a week at other times.

If the large numbers in which plays were put on the market in certain years oblige us to presume that they were obtained directly from the Companies of Players, as the only holders of plays who could supply them in this wholesale fashion, it is still part of my case that pirates existed and were occasionally successful. In the light of recently acquired knowledge it is interesting to note how these casual

IN SHAKESPEARE'S DAY 43

depredations were resisted. Until lately it was generally assumed that James Roberts was the most audacious of the pirates. The assumption was curiously hasty, because Roberts was in possession of two special privileges, and it was the unprivileged men whose financial straits led them to take dangerous risks in order to obtain work. One of Roberts's privileges, shared with Richard Watkins, was for printing all almanacks and prognostications; the other, obtained by marrying the widow of John Charlewood, the original grantee, was for printing all play bills. This would necessarily bring him into close touch with the players, and to suppose that he was at the same time openly robbing, or trying to rob, them, is unreasonable. Some ground for suspecting Roberts seemed to be offered by the occurrence of the words 'Printed by J. Roberts' on the title-pages of editions of *The Merchant of Venice* and *Midsummer Nights Dream* bearing the same date (1600) as those which he printed respectively for Thomas Heyes and Thomas Fisher; but now that (I hope I may say) it has been proved that these editions were not printed by him and only came into existence nineteen years later, there is nothing to hinder us from regarding him as an agent for the players, a part very well suited to the printer of their bills. When therefore we find that on four occasions Roberts entered plays on the Stationers' Register with a proviso that they should not be printed until he had produced better authority, instead of regarding him as a would-be pirate baffled by the exceptional caution of the authorities at Stationers' Hall, we may admit the probability that he was entering them in the interest of the players in order to postpone their publication till it could not injure the run of the play and to make the task of the pirates more difficult[1].

With the entries by Roberts we must mention two still more significant ones under the heading 'My lord Chamberlens mens plaies Entred.' The first of these is undated, and registers *A moral of clothe breches and velvet hose*, and an *Allarum to London*, with side-notes referring to the entries by Roberts on 27th and 29th May [1600] quoted above; the second, dated '4 Augusti,' reads:

> As you like yt, a booke
> Henry the ffift, a booke
> Every man in his humour, a booke
> The Commedie of muche Adoo about
>   nothing, a booke

to be staied.

Here we have the 'Lord Chamberlen's men' themselves taking action with the Stationers' Company direct, despite the fact that they had no status in it, to protect their own property. The fact that the Stationers permitted them to do this is significant of the influence which as the Lord Chamberlain's servants they possessed; the fact that they were driven to do it is significant also, for it shows indisputably that the danger of piracy was real, and enables us to be pretty sure that one or more acts of piracy had already been committed.

[1] On 27th July, 1598, he entered in this way *The Merchant of Venice*, 'provided it be not printed without licence first had from the Lord Chamberlain'; on 27th May, 1600, 'A moral of Cloth Breeches and Velvet Hose as it is acted by my Lord Chamberlain's servants... provided that he is not to put it in print without further and better authority,' and two days later *The Allarum to London*, 'provided that it be not printed without further authority'; lastly, on 7th February, 1603, *Troilus and Cressida* 'as it is acted by my Lord Chamberlain's men... when he hath gotten sufficient authority for it.'

IN SHAKESPEARE'S DAY 45

That some of Shakespeare's plays were pirated we have evidence in a passage from the address in the Folio of 1623, 'To the great Variety of Readers,' which has been quoted, or quoted from, 'ad nauseam,' but which we must quote once more. 'It had bene,' write Heminge and Condell, or whoever held the pen for them:

> It had bene a thing, we confesse, worthie to haue bene wished, that the Author himselfe had liu'd to haue set forth, and ouerseen his owne writings; But since it hath bin ordain'd otherwise, and he by death departed from that right, we pray you do not envie his Friends, the office of their care, and paine, to haue collected & publish'd them; and so to haue publish'd them, as where (before) you were abus'd with diuerse stolne, and surreptitious copies, maimed and deformed by the frauds and stealthes of iniurious impostors, that expos'd them: euen those are now offer'd to your view cur'd, and perfect of their limbes; and all the rest, absolute in their numbers, as he conceiued them. Who, as he was a happie imitator of Nature, was a most gentle expresser of it. His mind and hand went together: And what he thought, he vttered with that easinesse, that wee haue scarse receiued from him a blot in his papers.

Here we have two positive statements (1) that purchasers had been 'abus'd with diuerse stolne and surreptitious copies, maimed and deformed by the frauds and stealthes of iniurious impostors that expos'd them,' and (2) that 'even those' plays were now presented 'cur'd, and perfect of their limbes.' The whole point of the paragraph is that the pirated plays had been maimed and deformed in the process, and were now cured and perfected. While, therefore, it is good evidence of piracy, it only applies to plays of which the Quartos have bad texts and the Folio good ones. Now the plays of which the Quarto texts are, by common consent, strikingly inferior to those of the First Folio, are:

Romeo and Juliet. Printed by John Danter, 1597.
Henry the Fifth. Printed by Thomas Creede for Tho. Millington and John Busby, 1600.
The Merry Wives of Windsor. Printed by T. C. [i.e. Thomas Creede] for Arthur Johnson, 1602.
Hamlet, Prince of Denmark. Printed for N. L. [i.e. Nicholas Ling] and John Trundell, 1603. The printer being identifiable as Valentine Sims.

To which may be added as a bad text, though excluded from the First Folio, *Pericles, Prince of Tyre*, printed for Henry Gosson, 1609.

Now if we put these five plays as a provisional class, marked out as such by the verdicts of Shakespeare editors holding every variety of view on the subject of piracy, and if we put on the other side all the other First Editions in Quarto, including two first editions of a different text of *Romeo and Juliet*, and a different text of *Hamlet*, are there any other marked characteristics by which the two groups are differentiated?

In the first place we find, to our comfort, that not one of the bad texts was used as a basis for printing the play in the First Folio. So that if there were no other 'Stolne and surreptitious' editions than these, the editors of the Folio were as good as their word, and had presented 'Euen those' plays which had originally been pirated 'cur'd and perfect of their limbes.'

On the other hand, of the fourteen texts in our other class no fewer than twelve were used as the

IN SHAKESPEARE'S DAY 47

basis of the First Folio text, the two exceptions being the *Second Part of Henry IV*, of which the Quarto prints an earlier acting version and the Folio a later one, and *Othello*, of which the Quarto was only published in 1622, when the arrangements for the First Folio must have been already made.

In the second place, we note that not one of the five plays in what (for convenience and without prejudice) we may call the pirated group was entered on the Stationers' Register by its publishers, although Arthur Johnson was clever enough to get a man of straw to enter the *Merry Wives* and assign it to him on the same day, thus securing the copyright.

On the other hand, of the fourteen plays in our other group no fewer than twelve were duly entered before publication on the Stationers' Register, the two exceptions being *Romeo and Juliet*, of which an edition 'Newly corrected, augmented, and amended' was published by Cuthbert Burby in 1599, and *Loves Labors Lost*, of which an edition 'Newly corrected and augmented' had been published, also by Burby, the previous year. As a licence was only required for new books the existence of a previous (pirated) edition enabled Burby to save his sixpence in the case of *Romeo and Juliet*, and it seems more than probable that his similar saving in the case of *Loves Labors Lost* and also the words on the title-page 'Newly corrected and augmented' are to be explained by Danter having published a pirated edition of this also, though no trace of it now remains.

On 22nd January, 1607, both *Romeo and Juliet* and *Loves Labors Lost* were entered as the copies of Nicholas Ling 'by direccõn of a Court and with consent of Master Burby in wrytinge.' Thus all the fourteen good texts were eventually entered on the Register. On these grounds it is submitted that an entry in the Stationers' Register may be taken as *prima facie* evidence that a play was honestly purchased from the players to whom it belonged, while the absence of an entry or entry and immediate transfer, as in the case of the *Merry Wives*, points to a play being printed without the players' leave, or in other words 'pirated.'

In the light of this evidence let us now try to reconstruct the story of the publication of Shakespeare's plays in Quarto. On 6th February, 1594, soon after the time that many plays were being sold, as we must believe, by the players owing to the theatres being closed because of the plague, John Danter entered *Titus Andronicus* for his copy, and before the end of the year printed an edition which was sold by Edward White and Thomas Millington. Whether this should be reckoned a Shakespeare Quarto or not, literary critics must decide; but as it was printed as his in the Folio of 1623 it comes within our survey. In 1597 Danter, who had in the intervening three years gone down in the world (his press had been seized in 1596), printed a pirated edition of *Romeo and Juliet*, and very probably a similarly pirated edition of *Loves Labors Lost*. Finding themselves thus attacked, the players, lest more plays should go the same way, sold to Andrew Wise the right to print three of Shakespeare's Chronicles, *Richard II*, *Richard III*, and *Henry IV, Part I*. On Danter's death, or possibly a little earlier on his damning himself past redemption by pirating the *Grammar and Accidence*, they gave Cuthbert Burby, whom we must regard as the first of their

IN SHAKESPEARE'S DAY 49

confidential publishers, good texts of *Loves Labors Lost* and *Romeo and Juliet*, which he brought out in 1598 and 1599, thereby regaining the copyright. About the same time, on 22nd July, 1598, they instructed James Roberts, the printer of their play-bills, to prevent the piracy of *The Merchant of Venice* by entering it on the Stationers' Register with the proviso 'that yt bee not printed by the said James Robertes or anye other whatsoever without lycence first had from the Right honorable the lord Chamberlen.'

In 1600 the Chamberlain's men apparently had reason to fear piracy, and at the same time, owing to the Order in Council of 22nd June restricting their performances to two a week, were more inclined to sell. They therefore themselves, on 4th August, 'stayed' *As you like it*, *Henry V*, and *Much ado about Nothing*, only to find that *Henry V* had already been pirated by Thomas Millington and John Busby. *As you like it* they prevented from being printed at all, but they sold *Much Ado* to Andrew Wise and William Aspley, and with it *The second part of Henry IV*. They also sold the *Midsummer Night's Dream* to Thomas Fisher and sanctioned the *Merchant of Venice* being published by Thomas Heyes, the printing of this (and of the *Midsummer Night's Dream* also) being given to their play-bill printer, James Roberts, who had previously stayed for them the *Merchant of Venice*.

In January, 1602, when the Chamberlain's men were still in disgrace for having acted *Richard II* before the partisans of the Earl of Essex, John Busby the elder, who had previously pirated *Henry V*, successfully repeated the trick in the case of the *Merry*

Wives of Windsor, entering it on the Register on 18th January, and transferring it on the same day to Arthur Johnson. In the following July James Roberts entered on the Register *The Revenge of Hamlet*, and on 7th February, 1603, *Troilus and Cressida*, in the latter case with the old proviso 'to print when he hath gotten sufficient aucthority for it.' Roberts never printed *Troilus and Cressida* at all, and probably had no intention of printing *Hamlet*. Printed it was, however, though not (as has been believed) by him, but by Valentine Sims, and published by N. L. (i.e. Nicholas Ling) and John Trundell some time in 1603, or before Lady-Day, 1604. In this case the players seem to have condoned the attack, and Ling was allowed to publish a revised edition, which was printed for him by Roberts, and shortly afterwards took over the Shakespeare copyrights which had belonged to Cuthbert Burby.

After this Shakespeare's company, now the King's Majesty's Servants, had some years' freedom from piracy, partly owing to the fact that the censorship of plays was now more severe, and before entry in the Stationers' Register they had to be licensed by the censor, Sir George Buc. Being in the sunshine of the King's favour, and protected from piratical attack, they had no need to sell plays, and withheld them from the press much more rigorously. Nevertheless, on 26th November, 1607, *King Lear* was registered for their copy by Nathaniel Butter and John Busby in a singularly long and pompous entry, and duly printed from a playhouse copy the next year. It seems clear that the King's players consented to this, and yet as John Busby (if it was Busby senior who entered the play, as seems agreed) had robbed

IN SHAKESPEARE'S DAY 51

them twice before, and their policy was clearly against printing, it seems improbable that they did so willingly. I venture to hazard the suggestion that Busby may have been in a position to annoy them by reprinting the old play of *King Leir* (with an 'i'), which Simon Stafford, a printer frequently in trouble, had entered and printed when *Lear* (with an 'a') was first being acted in 1605. It is interesting to note that in the following May (20th May, 1608), Roberts being no longer in business, Edward Blount, subsequently the publisher of the First Folio, registered *Pericles* and *Anthony and Cleopatra*, and thereafter showed no more eagerness to publish them than Roberts had done in the case of *Troilus*.

As it happened, *Troilus* was the next play to appear, being re-entered on 28th January, 1609, to Richard Bonion and Henry Walleys and printed the same year. It seems not impossible that this edition was permitted by the players at Shakespeare's request in continuance of an old feud with George Chapman, who was then about to publish the first twelve books of his translation of the *Iliad*. On the other hand, despite Blount's precautionary entry, 'The late and much admired Play called Pericles, Prince of Tyre' was pirated in 1609 by Henry Gosson, a small publisher, who dealt chiefly in ballads, broadsides, and other popular literature. According to Thomas Heywood, it was a little before this that some of his plays had been 'coppied by the eare,' and had their plot drawn by stenography, 'scarce one word trew,' and *Pericles* seems to have come into the hands of Gosson in some such manner, let us hope 'accidentally.'

Finally, in 1622 Thomas Walkley thought it

worth while, and was allowed to print *Othello* separately in Quarto, when the great Folio was already in progress, and this brings to a close our story. In this we show the players selling plays when they cannot act them, attacked by a pirate, selling more old plays and trying to safeguard others by precautionary entries. Attacked again, when in disgrace at Court, they again resort to selling and staying. After five years' immunity we find them, in 1608 and 1609, selling *King Lear* (perhaps to a blackmailer), once more resorting to precautionary entries, losing *Pericles*, and then regaining control of their property, and suffering no more losses. Is not this a more probable picture than that which represents men like Burby, Roberts, and Blount as playing the pirates' game, and the servants of the Lord Chamberlain and of the King's Majesty himself as sitting down tamely under their attacks?

THE MANUSCRIPTS OF SHAKESPEARE'S PLAYS

IN our last paper we tried to reconstruct, in a reasonable and human manner, the story of how the Company of Players to which Shakespeare belonged met, as best they could, the successive attempts to pirate his plays. We found them after each piracy trying to protect certain plays, presumably those which they were then acting, by causing them to be entered on the Stationers' Register, so that no pirate should be able to obtain the copyright of them. That these entries in several instances were not followed by the appearance of an edition seemed to justify us in believing that their sole object was to defeat the pirates. On the other hand when the company had in their possession plays still saleable, but not being performed, still more when the theatre was closed owing to plague, or the number of performances was restricted in deference to Puritan complaints, we held that it might have been good business to sell plays to the best advantage, more especially if the pirates had been busy and there was any uncertainty as to what plays they had got hold of. We submitted on these lines that the company sold during Elizabeth's reign and the first year of James I eight plays by Shakespeare to friendly publishers, and in three other cases asserted their rights after a piracy by putting out better texts. After their position as the King's servants was secured they were only induced by special reasons in each case to permit the publication

54 THE MANUSCRIPTS OF

of *Lear* and *Troilus*, and just before the appearance of the Folio of 1623 sanctioned a quarto edition of *Othello*. Altogether they handed over to the printers the texts of fourteen plays. We have now to consider, from our bibliographical standpoint, what sort of texts these were, and what usually happened to a playwright's manuscript from the moment that it first left his hand to the time when it was used to light a fire or play some mysterious part in baking mackerel or lining a pie.

From the bibliographical standpoint a play of Shakespeare's is not a masterpiece of dramatic poetry, but so many sheets of paper with so much writing on them, by the aid of which actors had to say their words, and subsequently printers had to reproduce what the author wrote. After which, if the actors continued to say their words and the play was reprinted, more or less frequently, the bibliographer wants to know with what aids this process went on. When we have done our best by piecing together evidence from different quarters, and in default of evidence by supposing everyone to have taken as little trouble and gone to as little expense as possible, whatever story we are able to construct will at best be the story of an average or normal play, and how far it applies accurately to the case of any individual play or plays in which we are interested is a matter on which there may or may not be specific evidence. We must walk humbly in this matter; but it is not humility but laziness to give up any attempt to reconstruct what happened, because the task is difficult and we know that we can only attain partial success. Every editor of an old text is constantly, whether he realizes it or not, making various assumptions as to

SHAKESPEARE'S PLAYS 55

what happened in its progress from manuscript to print and from one edition to another, and to force ourselves to think out the whole process should at least give us a keener perception as to whether our assumptions are bibliographically possible or impossible.

A playwright has written a play for the Chamberlain's men. It will be better not to call the playwright Shakespeare before we are obliged, because we so often unconsciously assume that Shakespeare must always have been regarded as a person of special importance and his writings have been in some way specially treated, whereas when his plays first began to be printed it was apparently not thought worth while to put his name on their title-pages. Our anonymous playwright then has sold a play to the Chamberlain's men. Was that manuscript likely to have been in his own handwriting or a scrivener's? If it had been written for the company which Henslowe exploited the scrivener would be ruled out by the fact that the playwright, or playwrights, would have been paid so little and that, not improbably, by small advances, that they would certainly have grudged the scrivener his fee. In the case of the Chamberlain's men, who paid better and attracted the best writers, the weightiest objection to the scrivener would be the increased chance of piracy. If a scrivener were employed to make one copy, he might take the opportunity of making two. As it was, the players were exposed to some risks; for Greene was accused by the author of *A Defence of Cony-Catching*, 1592 (sig. C 3) of having sold his *Orlando Furioso* for twenty nobles to the Queen's players, and then, when they were in the country, to the Admiral's men for as much more, and Heywood asserts that some playwrights reserved a copy to sell to the booksellers behind the players' becks. However this may be, the scrivener would certainly have introduced a fresh possibility of loss.

As a basis for our doubts as to whether dramatists as a rule handed their plays to the companies in fair copies written for them by scriveners, we are not restricted to these *à priori* arguments. On 13th November, 1613, we find the industrious, but ever impecunious Daborne writing to Henslowe as to his tragedy on Machiavelli:

You accuse me with the breach of promise: trew it is I promysed to bring the last scean, which that you may see finished I send you the foul sheet & the fayr I was wrighting, as your man can testify, which if great busines had not prevented I had this night fynished... Howsoever I will not fayle to write this fayr and perfit the book, which shall not ly on your hands. (*Henslowe Papers*, ed. W. W. Greg, article 89, page 78.)

Here we see Daborne acting as his own copyist, making up the book of the play by instalments, as he found time, and sending his rough copy in advance when Henslowe grew impatient. It would be interesting to have this autograph manuscript and see what it looks like. Unfortunately it has not been preserved, but several plays by other contemporaries of Shakespeare have come down to us in their authors' own handwriting, and when we examine some of these two very important points come to light: (i) that, contrary to what might have been expected, the players were able to obtain the verdict of the Master of the Revels as to whether a play might be publicly acted, or not, by submitting to him the play as written

SHAKESPEARE'S PLAYS 57

by the author, or authors, sometimes in pretty rough manuscript, and with passages written on slips and pasted in; and (ii) that, again contrary to what might have been expected, plays endorsed with the licence for their public performance might be handed over to the prompter, and by him converted into prompt copies, without the 'play-house scrivener,' if such a person existed, being given a chance.

There are at the British Museum at least three plays extant in the autograph of their author or authors which also bear the endorsement of the Master of the Revels or his Deputy. These are:

(i) *The Book of Sir Thomas Moore*, of which Anthony Munday acted as the scribe, his manuscript probably including the work of other authors, while one of the additions is certainly in the hand of Dekker, and another almost certainly in that of Shakespeare. The signed play by Munday, *John à Kent and John à Cumber*, from which his writing in the 'Moore' manuscript was identified has part of its last leaf torn away, so that an endorsement may possibly have been written on this also.

(ii) Massinger's *Believe as you list* (1631).

(iii) *The Lancheinge of the Mary or the Seaman's Honest Wife*, a curious play in praise of the East India Company, by W. M., identified as William Mountford, with whose handwriting it agrees. This is endorsed by Sir Henry Herbert, 27 June, 1633.

Another play in the same manuscript (Egerton, 1994), as the last[1], *The Lady Mother* (confidently

[1] Since the first edition of these Lectures this Egerton Manuscript has been made the subject of an important article by Mr F. S. Boas printed in *The Library* (3rd series. Vol. VIII. 225–239). Mr Boas has shown that the fifteen plays it contains were almost certainly brought together by the

assigned by Mr Arthur Bullen to Glapthorne) is endorsed by William Blagrave, Herbert's deputy, 15th October, 1635, and appears to have been written out by a scrivener and corrected by the author.

The *Book of Sir Thomas Moore* has the name of an actor, Goodale, substituted for that of the part he plays, but the changes required by the licenser were so drastic that Dr Greg may well be right in believing that the idea of acting the play had to be abandoned, and if this is so we must attribute the use of Goodale's name to the author of this section of the play rather than to the prompter. Both *The Lancheinge of the Mary* and *The Lady Mother* are certainly prompt copies, and two other manuscript plays in the British Museum show clear signs of having passed through the hands both of the licenser and prompter. One of these, *Sir John Barnevelt* (Add. 18653), attributed to Fletcher and Massinger, has a sidenote beginning 'I like not this,' signed G. B., i.e., Sir George Buc, while the *Second Maidens Tragedy* in Lansdowne 807 owes its title to Buc, and

younger William Cartwright, actor and bookseller, who in 1635 was a member of the Revels Company, with which four of the plays can be connected by the occurrence in them of the names of minor actors instead of those of the characters which they represent. Two of these plays, *Edmund Ironsides* and a version of *Richard II*, Mr Boas attributes on the ground of style to 1590–1595, and another, Heywood's *The Captives*, had been acted by the Cockpit company in October, 1624. In the case of plays written so many years earlier and which still held the stage we should hardly expect the prompt-copy to be the original manuscript. It will be noted that the *Lancheinge of the Mary* and *The Lady Mother*, on which author, licenser and prompter seem all to have left their mark, were first brought out when the younger Cartwright was already a member of the company, and so had not had time enough to get worn out and replaced. The other plays in the volume have not yet been fully examined.

SHAKESPEARE'S PLAYS 59

bears his licence for its representation dated 1611. Both manuscripts were undoubtedly afterwards used as prompt copies.

This being the best light we can obtain as to the theatrical custom, have we any special information in the case of Shakespeare's plays? As we have seen, a curious vein of pessimism has caused many scholars, especially during the last thirty years, to enlarge the reference, in the preface to the First Folio, to 'diuerse stolne and surreptitious copies' from a verifiable statement, that even such plays as had been maimed in the quartos were presented in sound texts, into a general accusation casting the slur of surreptitiousness on all the quartos indiscriminately. On the other hand, save as a peg on which Ben Jonson hung a characteristic criticism, very little importance seems to be attached to the remarkable statement at the end of the same paragraph which, after praise of Shakespeare as 'a happie imitator of Nature' and 'a most gentle expresser of it,' proceeds 'His mind and hand went together: And what he thought, he vttered with that easinesse, that wee haue scarse receiued from him a blot on his papers.'

The importance of this statement, the justification for calling it remarkable, is that, if it has any meaning at all, it implies two things: first, that the Folio editors, as members of Shakespeare's Company, had received from him 'his papers,' i.e. autograph manuscripts of at least some of his plays; and secondly, that these autograph manuscripts were not 'fair copies,' such as Daborne and other authors were in the habit of delivering, but the text of the plays as he first wrote them down. Unless the papers were first drafts the claim made on Shakespeare's behalf on the ground of the absence of blots becomes ridiculous. The absence of blots from a scrivener's copy would prove nothing at all; therefore the papers must have been autograph. The absence of blots from an autograph 'fair' copy might be instanced as a proof of the writer's neatness, or accuracy, or willingness to take trouble, or even his affection for his fellows, and so forth; but by no logical gymnastics could it be quoted as a basis for the assertion that his mind and hand went together and what he thought he uttered with this 'easinesse' that is held up to admiration. Therefore, if the statement is to be allowed any meaning, the papers were not fair copies, but the original drafts.

The address in the First Folio 'to the great Variety of Readers,' from which we have been quoting, is a very tradesmanlike advertisement. The book 'is now publique,' Heminge and Condell write,

& you wil stand for your priuiledges wee know: to read and censure. Do so, but buy it first. That doth best commend a Booke, the Stationer saies. Then, how odde soeuer your braines be, or your wisedomes, make your licence the same, and spare not. Judge your sixe-pen'orth, your shillings worth, your five shillings worth at a time, or higher, so you rise to the iust rates, and welcome. But, what euer you do, Buy. Censure will not driue a Trade, or make the Jacke go.

This is poor enough stuff to offer some justification for regarding whatever follows as mere advertisement, and when we turn to the Dedication 'to the most noble and incomparable paire of Brethren,' the Earls of Pembroke and Montgomery, its heavy servility may confirm our ill impression. No doubt

SHAKESPEARE'S PLAYS 61

a handsome present was expected from the 'incomparable paire,' and the writers were ready to call Shakespeare's plays 'trifles' and make 'humble offer' of them to the dedicatees in order to get it. 'We haue observed,' they tell them naively, 'no man to come neere your Lordships but with a kind of religious address,' and customs having changed, their attempt to assume this 'religious' attitude repels us. But with a little sympathy we can understand both the advertisement and the obsequiousness, and arrive at a juster estimate of Heminge and Condell. The First Folio, with nearly a thousand pages of double-columned small type was a heavy venture for all concerned in it, and to obtain influential patronage and suggest to well-wishers quips by which they might shame the recalcitrant into buying may have seemed necessary business precautions. They should not make us doubt the sincerity of the assurance that the editors had taken up their task 'without ambition either of selfe-profit or fame: onely to keepe the memory of so worthy a Friend & Fellow aliue, as was our Shakespeare.' There is a ring of real affection about this phrase, which makes it incredible that the men who used it should on the next page have picked out a literary characteristic of Shakespeare's only to lie about it. So when Heminge and Condell[1] write: 'His mind and hand went together: And what he thought, he vttered with that easinesse, that we haue scarse receiued from him a blot on his papers,' we shall do well to believe that the autograph manu-

[1] Even if it should be proved beyond contradiction that the prefatory matter in the First Folio was written not by Heminge and Condell, but for them, the argument in this paragraph would hardly be affected, as a statement of this kind must surely have been inserted from their information.

scripts of some at least[1] of Shakespeare's plays had passed through the hands of Heminge and Condell, and that these contained the texts as they were first written down in the moment of composition.

On the authority of the editors of the First Folio we are thus justified in believing that Shakespeare, like Munday and Daborne and Massinger and other dramatists, brought his plays to the theatre in his own autograph. Heminge and Condell may only have seen the manuscripts of the later plays, but if Shakespeare avoided the scriveners when he was already rich and piracy had greatly abated, it is highly improbable that he employed them in his early days when the danger from piracy was much greater. In the absence of evidence to the contrary in the case of any individual play there is thus a bibliographical

[1] It has been pointed out that the title of the First Folio ('Mr William Shakespeares Comedies, Histories & Tragedies. Published according to the True Originall Copies') and still more the half-title ('The Workes of William Shakespeare, containing all his Comedies, Histories, and Tragedies: Truely set forth, according to their first *Originall*) suggest, and were probably intended to suggest, more than this 'some at least.' It is even argued that since they fraudulently suggest more than we can believe to be literally true, therefore all the editors' statements on the subject must be dismissed as untrustworthy. It seems to me equally unsound to press a seventeenth century's editor's or publisher's statement, as it might be legitimate to press a twentieth century one, so as to make it responsible for the extreme limit of what it seems to say, and to treat it as meaning nothing at all. Putting aside the point that the title and half-title may exhibit Ed. Blount liberally interpreting the assurances of Heminge and Condell, I think the statements mean that a real effort had been made to correct the corruptions of the later quartos and to substitute good texts for the pirated ones, and I think that in this sense they are true. But they have not the personal note which I find in the reference to Shakespeare's 'papers.'

presumption that it reached the players in the author's original autograph manuscript.

But in the case of other plays we have examined we find that the original manuscript was taken to the Master of the Revels for his consent to its being publicly acted, and that when this consent was endorsed on it the same manuscript was used as a prompt-copy. If this course was followed in the case of Shakespeare's manuscripts our case is complete, for there is a considerable body of evidence, which is as strong as regards some of Shakespeare's plays as any others, that when a play was printed by anyone except a pirate, it was the text of the prompt-copy that was set up. The evidence consists in the survival of stage-directions of a certain kind, and to explain it we must set forth the different sources from which the annotations which we lump together under this general name, stage-directions, could take their rise.

In writing out a play, for his own convenience as well as that of the players, a dramatist would naturally insert exits and entrances, in order to show who at any moment was on the stage. He might also, though as to this there was no uniformity, describe any action with which the player was to accompany his words. Possibly in some cases, if he were familiar with the theatre, he might use the same technical language as a prompter, so that Shakespeare himself, in the scene in the wood in the *Midsummer Night's Dream*, may have written the directions, 'Enter a Faerie at one doore and Robin goodfellow at another,' 'Enter the King of Fairies at one doore, with his traine; and the Queen at another with hers,' the 'doors,' of course, being those of the stage, not of the wood. Moreover, as Mr Greg has pointed out with reference to *Sir Thomas Moore*, the playwright would be almost as likely as the prompter to substitute the name of the actor for whom a part had been written for that of the part itself. In any case, however, when the manuscript reached the playhouse the prompter would go over it and insert in the margin any further directions needed for the performance, more especially as to the provision of stage properties or as to music, shouts, knocks, or other noises to be made in the room behind the stage, which was compendiously indicated by the word 'within.' For our present purpose, if the author's manuscript became the prompt-copy, whether any given direction was made by author or prompter is all one.

When a play was put into print the prompter's notes, whether written by himself or the author, as distinct from the descriptive notes, should in all cases have been either omitted or translated into descriptive phrases. Fairly often, however, one or more in a play is printed in its original form, and thus betrays the nature of the copy from which the printed text was set up. Thus, in the 1599 Quarto of *Romeo and Juliet*, although in Act I. Scene iv. we get the descriptive note 'Musick playes and they dance,' later on in the play we get such characteristic prompter's notes as 'Enter Romeo and Juliet aloft. Play Musicke'; or again, 'Enter Will Kemp' (the name of an actor, here substituted for his part), and 'Whistle boy.' So in the *Midsummer Night's Dream*, besides the directions as to the 'doors' at which the fairies are to enter in the wood, in III. ii. 85 we find the prompter's reminder to Demetrius, 'Ly down.' So also in *Much Ado about Nothing*, we find

SHAKESPEARE'S PLAYS 65

the names of the actors Kemp and Cowley, and in the *Second Part of Henry IV* that of Sincklo, substituted for the characters they had to play.

In the plays first printed in the Folio, in those at the beginning of each of the three sections Comedies, Histories, and Tragedies, the prompter's notes have usually been edited away; but in other plays we find several instances of the substitution of actors' names for their parts, and 'within' is almost uniformly used for anything done behind the scenes, so that in the Porter's speech in *Macbeth*, the note 'knocking within' is applied to Macduff's knocks on the outer gate. Also in the *Second Part of Henry VI*, III. ii. 146, the prompter's note, 'Bed put forth,' reveals to us the primitive stage management, which thrust forth a bed, with Gloucester's body on it, into the middle of the stage, instead of having it ceremoniously brought in, according to the directions in modern editions, 'Exit Warwick' and 'Re-enter Warwick and Others bearing Gloucester's body on a bed.'

If, as has been shown, there is a high probability that the prompt-copy of any of Shakespeare's plays would be written in the author's autograph; and if, as has also been shown, we know that the text of many of his plays, both of those printed in Quarto and of others which first appeared in the Folio of 1623, was derived from prompt-copies, we can only escape from admitting the probability that some, at least of Shakespeare's plays were set up directly from his own manuscript by supposing that now at last the scrivener was given a job, and that a scrivener's copy intervened between the printer and Shakespeare's autograph.

It may be said in support of this supposition that

if the players had handed over the actual prompt-copy to be printed they would have been left with no text of their own save such as could be reconstructed from the actors' parts. But the force of this objection is broken by the clear evidence which can be produced that copies of authorized Quartos were used in the theatre as prompt-copies. Thus, in the Folio text of *Much Ado about Nothing*, set up from the Quarto of 1600, while the substitution of the names of the actors Kemp and Wilson for Dogberry and Verges is retained, in Act II. scene iii. we find in the stage direction 'Enter Prince, Leonato, Claudio, and Jacke Wilson,' the name of Wilson, the singing man of the company, freshly substituted for that of Balthasar, who has to sing 'Sigh no more, ladies.' In the same way, in the *Midsummer Night's Dream*, for which the reprint of 1619 (dated 1600) was used for the Folio, this had clearly been used in the theatre, as two new and very obvious prompter's directions have crept in, namely in III. i. 116, 'Enter Piramus [i.e. Bottom] with the Asse-head' (where only the prompter, who knew that there was only one Ass-head in the playhouse stock of properties, would have written '*the* Asse-head' instead of '*an* Ass-head' as in modern editions), and again in V. i. 134, where the direction for the entry of the clowns is preceded by the note 'Tawyer with a trumpet before them.'

A Shakespeare Quarto could easily have been printed in a month if the printer employed a journeyman and a fairly advanced apprentice, so that if the players saw the superior convenience of a printed prompt-copy, and were not (as we may be sure) acting the plays at the time they sold them, no in-

SHAKESPEARE'S PLAYS 67

convenience would have arisen from their parting with their manuscript prompt-copy to the printer.

Another objection which suggests itself is that the players would be bound to keep in their archives the manuscript signed by the 'Master of the Revels,' in case they should be challenged for departing from the text approved. This seems to ignore the easy temper of English officialdom at all periods. A Spanish censor must needs have a notary initial every page of the manuscript submitted to him. Tilney, or Buc, or Herbert were content to write their licence at the end of the manuscripts already altered and added to, in some cases with slips containing additions pasted on to a leaf. By the time a play had been on the stage a year or two challenge would become less probable, and the fact that it had been licensed for printing should have been an ample answer. Even that grasping person, Sir Henry Herbert, when asked to re-license *The Winter's Tale* for revival in August, 1623, on Heminge reporting that the 'allowed book' (possibly the original manuscript) was missing, but giving his word 'that there was nothing prophane added or reformed' (*sic*), returned the play without a fee. On the other hand, it is intrinsically probable that, for obtaining the original licence to print, production of the signed manuscript would have been helpful even in Elizabeth's day, while in the next century this was probably indispensable.

On the whole, then, it seems reasonable to believe that in the case of a play printed after having been regularly entered in the Stationers' Register there is a high probability that a prompt-copy would be supplied to the printer; and there is a further high probability that such a prompt-copy would be the manuscript handed over to the players by the author; and yet a further high probability that this manuscript would be in the author's autograph. The highest probability is only a large fraction of a complete proof, and when three fractions are multiplied together they diminish very rapidly. It would need the odds in each case to be as four to one to leave us at the end of our three probabilities with anything more than an even chance. Perhaps it will be wise not to claim more than this even chance that the text of any given play reached the printer of the Quarto in Shakespeare's autograph; but in view of Heminge and Condell's statement as to the receipt of Shakespeare's 'papers,' the use of other autograph manuscripts for prompt-copies, the evidence that quartos of Shakespeare's plays were based on prompt-copies, and the occurrence of new traces of the prompter's hand in the First Folio text of plays printed from Quartos, there does not seem any reason why we should claim less than this.

It will probably be said that a claim which invites the belief that even half of the fourteen regularly entered Shakespeare Quartos were set up direct from Shakespeare's autograph manuscripts proves too much, because the texts of these first editions contain too many mistakes to stand in such immediate contact with their source. Not a few of these mistakes would be explained if we may believe, as it has been contended we should, that Shakespeare supplied the players not with revised copies, but with treacherously clean-looking rough ones. We have yet, moreover, to reckon with the Elizabethan printer, and the more closely we study the ways of Elizabethan printers, when employed on dramatic work, the more highly

SHAKESPEARE'S PLAYS 69

we shall rate his capacity for introducing any number of errors into the text supplied to him.

It has long been a commonplace among the textual critics of Shakespeare that in every Quarto edition subsequent to the First new mistakes are introduced, so that the text becomes progressively worse. In an extreme case, that of a probably hasty reprint of *Richard II*, taking the acceptance or rejection of a reading by the Cambridge editors as definitely marking it as right or wrong, a second quarto has been found to add about 180 per cent. of new errors to those originally made, so that it is nearly three times as incorrect. The case is exceptional, and it must also be remembered that although reprinting a reprinted edition is easier, and should therefore give a more correct result than printing from manuscript copy, as a matter of fact the very easiness of their task often makes compositors and correctors careless. It is also possible, or rather certain, that there are mistakes in the First Quartos which, because they leave the line in which they occur still intelligible, no one has suspected. In view, however, of the ceaseless stream of new errors poured into the text as first printed in every new edition, it is not possible to say in the case of an average First Quarto, duly entered on the Stationers' Register, that the blunders in it cannot all have been due to the printers, but that we must postulate the intervention of one or more copyists to share the blame. The proved inaccuracy of the printers suffices to account for all the faults.

We are not entirely dependent on the judgment of the Cambridge editors in estimating the blunder-making capacity of these printers. As is well known, in several plays of Shakespeare, and of Ben Jonson and other authors also, individual pages are found in two different states, one with certain errors in them, the other with these errors corrected. Where there is only one, or perhaps two, readings in question, it is possible in some cases that instead of speaking of an error and a correction we ought to speak of a right reading and a corruption, because it is certain that the inking-balls sometimes pulled one or more letters out of the forme, and that mistakes were made by these being incorrectly replaced. More commonly, however, and in some cases quite certainly, we can see that the pressmen had begun printing off a page before it had been fully corrected, and that on the master printer (who in a small printing-house, would usually act as his own corrector) coming in, the press was stopped and his corrections introduced in all the impressions of the page which remained to be pulled. Now on different impressions of one page of the first quarto of *Richard II* there are four, and on another as many as five, of these uncorrected and corrected readings. On B verso a word is omitted, a letter is added, and in two cases one word is substituted for another. On B_3 verso a word and a hyphen are omitted, a letter is omitted, one word is substituted for another, and two words caught from a previous line displace two others. That shows us what an Elizabethan compositor could do when his master was out. By the Cambridge standard the number of detected errors in the First Quarto of *Richard II* is less than one a page. Left to themselves, the compositors were capable of multiplying this fourfold, and we cannot tell how often this happened. That is a gloomy thought, and we are bound to

SHAKESPEARE'S PLAYS 71

remember that in the case of these two pages in *Richard II* the corrector did come back before the impression was completed, and was conscientious enough to stop the press to put things right as far as he could. But if any one contends that Elizabethan compositors could not have made the errors found in First Quartos without the help of copyists, it is well to bear in mind these instances of his error-making capacity.

We are thus emboldened to persist in our contention that in some cases Shakespeare's own autograph of a play may have been the copy supplied to its first printer, resting our case now on the four points: (i) that the manuscripts handed to the players were in Shakespeare's autograph; (ii) that in other cases we find an autograph manuscript used as a prompt-copy; (iii) that at least some of the First Quartos were set up from prompt-copies; (iv) that the proved inaccuracy of the printers allows us to assume an original quite as free from faults as an autograph copy supplied by Shakespeare was likely to be.

From the Quartos to the First Folio.

As regards the period from the first publication of a duly registered Quarto to the appearance of a play in the Folio of 1623, no editor, as far as I am aware, has ever propounded a formal theory that readings which appear for the first time in the later Quartos are based upon either a fresh consultation of the MS. already used, or access to a new one. As will be emphasized in our last paper, on 'the Improvers of Shakespeare,' editors have concerned themselves unnecessarily with the readings of the later Quartos and have admitted too many readings from them into their text: but they have done this rather on some muddle-headed plea that it all happened a long time ago, that the particular circumstances are very obscure, and that we must take good where we find it and be thankful, than with even the smallest attempt to show how any new authority was obtained. If an eighteenth century editor had had the courage to say that 'the Printer of the First Edition, fearing that he had not done Justice to the Untutored Charm of his Author, had kept the original MS. by him in the hope of Improving his Performance in another edition,' some one would doubtless have dealt satisfactorily with that editor before now. Surely he would have been confronted with a conspectus of all the changes introduced into any given second edition, and in the utter impossibility of contending that the performance as a whole had been improved, that it had not on the contrary been in every way worsened and depraved, a confession might have been extracted that the later Quartos could have had no other source for their most plausible readings than the wits of their own printers; for the press-correctors of these Quartos did undoubtedly use their wits in correcting blunders they found in the first editions, and sometimes with good success. The causes, however, of the great bulk of the variants introduced into the later Quartos seem to be those common to all copying and more especially the trick of carrying too many words at a time in the head. It has lately been pointed out to me by a master-printer that this tendency is especially active, and therefore especially dangerous, in reprinting from a printed text, in which the eye easily takes in a whole line at a glance, whereas the setting of the line would be a work of minutes, during

SHAKESPEARE'S PLAYS 73

which it would be easy for the memory to play tricks with one or more words. Besides these, of course, there are the usual transposition of letters, substitution of one letter for another, and other errors to which careless printers are liable. Not all of the printers of Quartos deserve to be stigmatized as careless; but many of them were very careless indeed.

When we come to the First Folio and begin to enquire into its relation with the Quartos, we find ourselves confronted with a series of readings which at first sight seem decisive against any new manuscripts having been available for improving the text of these plays. Anyone can make mistakes when he is careless. But when we find old blunders being hidden up by commonplace tinkering instead of the true reading being restored, it seems a fair inference, since the tinkerers were obviously wide awake and taking trouble, that the producers of the First Folio were driven to tinker because no other course was possible, i.e. because they had no independent authority at hand by which a real correction could be made.

These cases arise where the text of a First Quarto is sound, but an error has been introduced in the second or some later one, and the reading of the First Folio is obviously a tinkering of this error. A couple of instances of this kind may be quoted from among the examples of progressive corruption cited by Malone in his admirable preface in 1790.

In 1 *Henry IV.*, V. iii. 11, Blunt answers the threats of Douglas with the words:

I was not born a yielder, thou proud Scot.

In the Quarto of 1613 the printer substituted for

the three syllables 'a yielder' the two syllables 'to yield,' thus producing the unmetrical line:

> I was not born to yield, thou proud Scot.

In the First Folio this is mended with absolute neatness by the substitution of 'haughty' for 'proud,' the line thus becoming

> I was not born to yield, thou haughty Scot.

If the Quarto of 1613 had disappeared this reading might have held its own, against that of the First Quarto, as a genuine alternative obtained from a new manuscript. But with the nine-syllabled line already in evidence in the Quarto of 1613 we can see that the line has been cleverly botched, and that instead of suggesting the existence of an alternative manuscript, it is strong evidence that no authoritative text was available, and therefore botching had to be resorted to.

Again in the first Quarto of *Richard III.*, I. i. 63-65, Richard assures Clarence:

> 'Tis not the king that sends you to the Tower:
> My lady Grey his wife, Clarence, 'tis she
> That tempers him to this extremity.

In the last of these lines the later quartos substituted the monosyllable 'tempts' for the dissyllable 'tempers,' thus reducing it to

> That tempts him to this extremity.

In the Folio the line is eked out to its proper length by the interpolation of an adjective, giving us:

> That tempts him to this harsh extremity.

With the history of the line before him no one can doubt that this is botching or tinkering, and it is a

SHAKESPEARE'S PLAYS 75

perfectly sound inference that the botcher or tinker in question cannot have had easy access to a manuscript recording the true reading, or he would not have cudgelled his brains with this sorry result.

We must not, however, underrate the complexity of the problem with which we are dealing.

Where a duly registered quarto had been published, the text of the First Folio was usually, though not always, set up from the latest edition of this on the market, this being of course the easiest and cheapest way of supplying the printer with copy.

But in almost every case the Folio text supplies a number of new readings, which, like most other things in the world, may be quite accurately classified under the three headings good, bad, and indifferent.

By a 'Good' reading in this classification is meant a reading undoubtedly Shakespeare's. By a 'Bad' reading, one that is undoubtedly not Shakespeare's, but either belongs to the class of the Folio readings botched up out of the errors of the later Quartos at which we have just been looking, or is an obvious misprint. Lastly, 'Indifferent' readings are those which may be a little better aesthetically than their alternatives, or a little worse; but which, because they make sense and grammar and scan, and crop up mostly in what may be called the lower levels of Shakespeare's verse, we cannot treat as impossible, while it is equally clear that we cannot treat them as possessing any certainty in their own right. If we can find ground for believing that the text of any play first printed in quarto was revised *as a whole* by the aid of a good manuscript, then for these indifferent readings we must follow the text of the Folio. If on the other hand no such revision took place, then we must print them as they stand in the First Quarto.

If in the case of a given play we are to suppose that a good manuscript existed and was used in improving the text of the late Quarto, who are we to suppose had the manuscript entrusted to him and used it for this purpose?

We may rule out of consideration the person, or persons, whom we may think of as exercising the general editorship. Their task must have been to get together the material, decide what was to be printed and what not, settle the order of the plays, and carry through two specific bits of work, which required special knowledge—the division of the plays into acts and scenes and the substitution, where necessary, of descriptive notes for the imperatives of the old stage-directions. They did not complete either of these jobs—Parts 2 and 3 of *King Henry VI* seem to have been sent to the printer without any general editing of this kind whatever; several plays are only divided into acts, not into scenes, and imperative stage-directions are found sporadically—and as the general editors obviously could not find time to attend to this business, it is impossible to imagine that they had the time or the patience to attend to the collation of the text.

It is quite clear that hired aid must have been called in and that the work done by these hired helpers must have been accepted as final. That is to say, if any better text, manuscript or printed, was used in preparing that of the late Quarto for the press, the hired man corrected a copy of the late Quarto by this with as much care and skill as he had to bestow, and the copy so corrected became the sole

SHAKESPEARE'S PLAYS 77

authority for the new text. Very probably the hired man was not engaged for proof-reading; but even if he had been, it would have been out of keeping with the whole atmosphere which surrounds the publication of Shakespeare's plays, if he had discarded the copy for which he himself was responsible, and read the proofs with the better authority which he had collated. Hence, whether the hired man of our (not unreasoned) imagination, or the press-corrector in Jaggard's printing-house had the last word in the matter, if a line were faulty in the copy prepared for press, the choice would lie between leaving it as it was and the gross botching of which instances have been given.

In the case of some plays the question to be solved may finally take the form, How far may we reasonably push our belief in the incompetence of the collator in order to explain a few good readings being introduced into the Folio text along with a crowd of bad ones? Sooner than postulate an inhumanly incompetent collator, it might be well to consider whether no source existed from which isolated good readings might be derived without any new manuscript having been available. If we can conceive of the prompter of the Globe Playhouse making haphazard manuscript corrections on his prompt-copy, we may find in this a source of exactly the kind we want. There is ample evidence (some of it has been quoted) that copies of the printed Quartos were used in the Playhouse as prompt-copies, and that these prompt-copies were used in preparing the Folio text, with the result that some of their manuscript stage-directions got into print. If a prompter could annotate a printed quarto with additional stage-directions for his own use, there seems no reason why he should not have brought the text of his copy into some kind of occasional conformity with any variations made by the actors whom he had to prompt. The actors would presumably still have at their disposal the original acting-parts. In so far as they had learnt these correctly they would restore true readings which the First Quarto had corrupted. In so far as they had not learnt their parts correctly they would from imperfect memory make mistakes very similar to those made by printers from trying to carry too many words at a time in their heads. In the first instance (if the prompter was interested) we have an explanation of the appearance of two or three good readings in the Folio text where nothing else suggests that recourse had been had to any new authority. In the second instance (again if the prompter was interested) we may perhaps find a means for transferring to other shoulders some of the blame for the frequent substitution of one word for another which now, if we refuse to postulate a new manuscript, rests with the printer of the Folio.

If such an hypothesis as has here been sketched were accepted, the number of plays first printed in Quarto, for which we should have to call in new manuscript authority to account for the Folio text, would be small indeed. It is, however, no part of the bibliographer's work to poach on literary preserves as regards individual plays. Our business is to try to think out in terms of pieces of paper what must have happened for a reading which can be accepted as Shakespeare's to have got into the printed text, subsequently to the First Edition. In view of the licence which Elizabethan printers allowed themselves, we

SHAKESPEARE'S PLAYS 79

must refuse to invoke manuscript authority for any changes, right or wrong, which might easily originate with the printer—with his common sense or ingenuity, if the changes may be adjudged right, with his very conspicuous carelessness if they are wrong. In the same spirit of economy we must refuse to assume the availability of a manuscript for the revision of the whole text of a play, unless adequate evidence is forthcoming that the whole text was in fact revised. As a way of escape from such extravagance the alternative has here been proposed of haphazard corrections on a printed prompt-copy. But it must be constantly borne in mind that different plays may have had different fortunes. We are bound to suppose that the players as a rule took the cheapest and safest course; but it would be rash indeed to assume that they did so invariably, and that an additional transcript was never made and preserved and came in useful in 1623. All we have tried to do in this paper is to think out the problem in general terms, and trust the application to Shakespeare's editors, who hitherto have left the bibliographical side of the problem—the passing from hand to hand of pieces of paper—very imperfectly developed. On these lines we submit that it is bibliographically probable that some of the First Quarto Editions of Shakespeare's plays were printed from the author's own autograph manuscript, which had previously been used as a prompt-copy; that the actors replaced their manuscript prompt-copy by a copy of the printed Quarto, which in its turn received additional stage-directions and also readings representing some of the variants which were adopted by individual actors; that in 1622 a copy of the last Quarto on the market was sent to the playhouse to be roughly collated with the printed prompt-copy; and that the copy so corrected was the source of the Folio text of a normal play originally printed in a duly registered Quarto.

It may be added that in November, 1915, when this paper was read as a Sandars Lecture at Cambridge, I was applying this theory to the case of Shakespeare's *King Richard II*; readers of the introduction to the facsimile of the unique copy of the Third Quarto owned by Mr W. A. White, of New York (*A New Shakespeare Quarto*, London, Quaritch, 1916), must judge with what success.

THE IMPROVERS OF SHAKESPEARE

IN our third paper we tried to establish bibliographically what was the normal history of the text of Elizabethan plays from the time the playwright handed his manuscript to the players; we then enquired what special evidence we had in the case of Shakespeare's plays, and finally applied the theories we constructed to the history of his text down to the publication of the Folio of 1623. We shall devote the first part of this our last paper to three deductions of some importance arising out of this survey.

I. The first of these is that, from our bibliographical standpoint, the readings of any edition of a play of Shakespeare's subsequent to the First duly registered Quarto cannot have any shred of authority, unless a reasonably probable case can be made out for access having been obtained to a new manuscript, or its equivalent. And to construct such a case all the variants in the edition must be brought together and considered as a whole.

Editors of Shakespeare, even the best editors of Shakespeare, have been too ready to accept or reject variants on what they would call 'their individual merits'; and they have yielded, consciously or unconsciously, to the illusion that if a first edition printed (say) in 1597 is a good authority, a second edition printed within a year or two is also an authority, though perhaps not quite of equal weight.

THE IMPROVERS

A printed text cannot be invested with authority merely by an early date on its title-page. The authority can only come to it by derivation from the original manuscript, and if this derivation is simply and solely through a previous printed edition, then a reading in the second edition can have no authority whatever as against a reading in the first[1]. It may be right, as any conjectural emendation may be right; but it must be judged as a conjectural emendation, and on precisely the same footing as if it had been made a week ago.

The point is so obvious that it seems superfluous to labour it, but with the honourable exception of Malone, it has been almost uniformly neglected by Shakespeare's editors.

Theobald arranged his list of the editions known to him under the three headings:

>Editions of Authority,
>Editions of Middle Authority,
>Editions of no Authority.

He did this, doubtless, for the pleasure of making his third class, the editions of no authority, consist

[1] There is a seeming, though not a real, exception to this rule in the case of a reading in a second edition which follows a correction introduced into the text of the first edition after part of the copies of the sheet in which it occurs had already been printed off. Thus in *Richard II*, I. ii. 70, Q² rightly reads 'heare' as against the misprint 'cheere' in the British Museum (Huth) and Capell copies of Q¹, and, it was only after nearly half a century of controversy that 'heare' was discovered in the Huntingdon (Devonshire) copy. If more copies of Q¹ of *Richard III* are discovered one of them should surely contain the missing line and a half (I. i. 101 *sq.*) which at present seem to have been introduced for the first time in Q². It will be noted that it is only in cases where the extant copies of a first quarto are very few that this curious case can arise.

OF SHAKESPEARE 83

of those of Rowe and Pope. His second class contained the Third Folio and the Quartos printed between 1623 and the Restoration. But how did these later quartos acquire the Middle Authority which he ascribes to them? In so far as they were accurate reprints of the First registered Quarto, if every copy of that had been destroyed they might have taken its place. But as long as that remains they are purely negligible. And this applies with almost equal completeness to most of the editions included in Theobald's highest class, as Editions of Authority. These comprise all the Quartos, of which he knew, printed before 1623, and the First and Second Folios. It would be perhaps too much to say that a Quarto of 1615 is no better than a Quarto of 1655, because the latter will certainly have accumulated some more errors, and the Quarto of 1615, moreover, may be of considerable interest in determining for a given play the value of the First Folio. But as against a reading in a First Quarto, the authority which a variant derives from having been printed within one year, ten years, or forty years of it, is in every case the same, because in every case it is *nil*.

Just as, so long as a copy of the first edition of a good Quarto exists, all the later quarto editions have no value for the construction of a text; so, as long as a copy of the First Folio remains, the three later Folios have no textual importance. In criticizing Theobald's table of editions, Dr Johnson expressed this with his usual sturdy common sense:

In his enumeration of editions (he writes of Theobald) he mentions the two first folios as of high, and the third folio as of middle authority; but the truth is that the first

84 THE IMPROVERS

is equivalent to all [the] others, and that the rest only deviate from it by the printer's negligence. Whoever has any of the folios has all, excepting those diversities which mere reiteration of editions will produce. I collated them all at the beginning, but afterwards used only the first.

The importance of the later Quartos printed before 1623, and of the three later Folios, is purely genealogical. Had none of the later Quartos been preserved, we should have been obliged to debit to the First Folio as original errors, all the bad readings which it took over from the later Quartos. On the one hand, the credit of the Folio would have been unjustly depreciated; on the other hand, various easy readings introduced by the later Quartos would have been invested with whatever authority the Folio text for the play in which they occur may possess. But when once the errors borrowed by the Folio from the later Quartos have been eliminated, only the First Quartos and the First Folio have any textual value.

The genealogical importance of the later Folios is of much the same kind. It arises from the fact that the Fourth Folio being the easiest and cheapest to buy and also the most modern in its spelling was the copy which Rowe sent to the printer, after he had tinkered it at his pleasure. Pope used Rowe's text as his 'copy' to print from; Theobald used Pope's, and so on. It may be doubted whether any edition of Shakespeare's works (with the possible exception of Capell's) has ever been wholly printed from manuscript. That of 1623 was printed partly from manuscript, partly from the printed quartos. Probably every subsequent edition has been set up from some earlier printed text, some of the misprints in which will almost certainly be carried over into the new edition despite editorial care. Many of the readings of the Fourth Folio were thus inadvertently adopted by Rowe, and the Fourth Folio and its two immediate predecessors are thus necessary to a right understanding of the eighteenth century texts. But it must be said again and again that as authorities for ascertaining what Shakespeare himself actually wrote, no editions can have any shred, jot or tittle of value except the First Quartos[1], and the First Folio.

While it is true that the eighteenth century editors who started the editorial tradition as to Shakespeare's text had not all the bibliographical data before them, nor even a complete set of the First Quartos, their tendency to treat all the later Quartos and later Folios as in some degree authoritative was due much less to ignorance than to their desire to improve their text. It is a little lamentable that nowhere can we find this standpoint more clearly stated than in the words of Edward Capell, to whom Shakesperian criticism is so heavily indebted.

Listen to what he writes in the Introduction to his audaciously entitled edition of 'Mr. William Shakespeare his Comedies Histories and Tragedies, set out by himself [!] in quarto, or by the Players his Fellows in folio, and now faithfully republish'd from those Editions, in ten Volumes octavo':

It is said a little before,—that we have nothing of his in writing; that the printed copies are all that is left to guide us; and that those copies are subject to numberless

---

[1] Of course where there are two texts as in *Romeo and Juliet*, the First Quarto of each counts for whatever it may be worth. So also as regards the deposition scene the 1608 edition of *Richard II* counts as a First Quarto.

THE IMPROVERS

imperfections, but not all in like degree: our first business then, was—to examine their merit, and see on which side the scale of goodness preponderated, which we have generally found, to be on that of the most ancient: It may be seen in the Table, what Editions are judg'd to have the preference among those plays that were printed singly in quarto; and for those plays, the text of those Editions is chiefly adher'd to: in all the rest, the first folio is follow'd; the text of which is by far the most faultless of the Editions in that form; and has also the advantage in three quarto plays, in 2 *Henry IV*, *Othello* and *Richard III*.

Up to this point nothing could be more sound, and the service which Capell was rendering, in so far as he based his text on the earliest editions instead of trusting to collation to eliminate the faults of the later ones, was very great. Unhappily he proceeds:

Had the editions thus follow'd been printed with carefulness, from correct copies, and copies not added to or otherwise alter'd after those impressions, there had been no occasion for going any further: but this was not at all the case, even in the best of them; and it therefore became proper and necessary to look into the other old editions, and to select from thence whatever improves the Author, or contributes to his advancement in perfectness, the point in view throughout all this performance: that they do improve him was with the editor an argument in their favour; and a presumption of genuineness for what is thus selected, whether additions or differences of any other nature; and the causes of their appearing in some copies and being wanting in others, cannot now be discover'd, by reason of the time's distance, and defect of fit materials for making the discovery.

As if to put his method of procedure beyond any possibility of doubt, he concludes:

...Without entering further in this place into the

OF SHAKESPEARE 87

reasonableness or even necessity of so doing, he does for the present acknowledge,—that he has everywhere made use of such materials as he met with in other old copies, which he thought improv'd the editions that are made the ground-work of the present text (pp. 21-22).

Capell's present critic has a personal reason for being moderate in his strictures, because (some thirty years ago) moved by a laudable desire to win more readers for Chaucer's *Canterbury Tales* without entering on the slippery paths of modernizing, he laboriously picked out from the seven texts published by the Chaucer Society the spellings easiest to a modern reader in every line, and thus produced an edition for the spelling of every word of which there was early manuscript authority, but which certainly did not present the words as Chaucer wrote them. Had Capell, in order to popularize Shakespeare without committing himself to wholesale tinkering, announced that he had accepted the emendations or improvements proposed by Shakespeare's contemporaries, and those only, it might still have been questioned whether what he did was worth doing, but he would not have introduced any fundamental confusion into editorial ideals. As it was, he did introduce, or at least help to perpetuate, confusion, by asserting his right to correct original editions by others that were merely old, and by the specious suggestion that the fact of a new reading being (in editorial eyes) an 'improvement' carried with it a 'presumption of genuineness.' As bibliographers we must protest that it is not mere age, but proof of independent access to a source, that gives an edition authority, while with any other aim than that of ascertaining what was on the sheets of paper which Shakespeare wrote and handed to the players we can have nothing to do, unless we find evidence of his personal revision of this original text. That is our first point, and it brings us into collision with almost every editor of Shakespeare, even (although to an exceptionally slight extent) with the honoured editors of the Cambridge text.

II. The second deduction we have to draw is that, although it is probable that the first authorized printers of any play by Shakespeare had but scant respect for such spelling, punctuation and system of emphasis capitals as they found in their copy, yet as it requires less mental effort to follow copy mechanically than consciously to vary from it, we are bound to believe that in these matters, as well as in the words of the text, the first authorized edition of any play is likely to be nearer than any other to what the author wrote.

In regard to these matters we cannot, as we should like to do, claim that we still have Dr Johnson on our side. 'In restoring the author's works to their integrity,' wrote the Doctor, 'I have considered the punctuation as wholly in my power; for what could be their care of colons and commas, who corrupted words and sentences [?].' The argument which underlies this charmingly alliterative sentence, which, however, with curious ill luck ends with a full stop instead of a mark of interrogation—the argument is perfectly sound. It *is* highly probable that such punctuation as Shakespeare bestowed on his manuscript is less, perhaps much less, faithfully reproduced, than his words. But what proportion of Shakespeare's words have we any reason to believe were corrupted by his first printers? Even on a pessimistic view

OF SHAKESPEARE 89

certainly not one in a hundred. If his punctuation, therefore, were ten times as carelessly reproduced as his words, nine out of ten of the stops in a first authorized Quarto would be as Shakespeare wrote them. As against Dr Johnson this seems a very fair argument, though no doubt he would have 'downed' it more or less successfully. As a matter of fact, we have to take into consideration quite another probability, the probability that Shakespeare, unless it definitely occurred to him that he would like to have a speech delivered in a particular way, was himself much too rapid a writer to be at all careful about his stops. If this is so, his first printers, instead of simply following his punctuation faithfully, must often have been called upon to supply the lack of it as best they could; so that all numerical estimates of their fidelity must go by the board.

If, however, we ask whether there is any reason to believe (*a*) that it did sometimes occur to Shakespeare that he would like to have a speech delivered in a particular way, (*b*) that he could and did indicate this by punctuation, and (*c*) that this punctuation, at least in some cases, is quite faithfully reproduced, the answers we can offer to these questions do not encourage us to acquiesce at all cheerfully in Johnson's assumption that the punctuation of the plays was 'wholly in [his] power.' By Johnson's day the punctuation which we find in Elizabethan books, more especially in plays, may be correctly described as a lost art. Dr Johnson might do what he pleased with colons and commas. He could make them help to show how a sentence of Shakespeare's should be parsed; but he could not make them show how it would be delivered by a great actor—because that might have interfered with the parsing. Now, in his little book on Shakespearian Punctuation, though his method of exposition may not in all respects win acceptance, Mr Percy Simpson has abundantly proved that what could not be done in Johnson's days could be done in Shakespeare's. Everyone interested not only in the Elizabethan drama, but in all the outburst of poetry from Tottell's *Miscellany* to Herrick, should buy and study Mr Simpson's book, which is published by the Clarendon Press for five shillings. It is only right to say, however, that he had been preceded in this field by Mr A. E. Thiselton, who, in a succession of separately printed notes to various plays of Shakespeare, had paid special attention to their punctuation and already discovered a method in what commentators have accounted the madness of that found in the early editions. Both Mr Simpson (to whom I owe my own conversion) and Mr Thiselton have presented their results mainly in terms of grammar and syntax. My own way of restating the facts as I understand them, is that in Shakespeare's day, at any rate in poetry and the drama, all the four stops, comma, semicolon, colon, and full stop, could be, and (on occasion) were, used simply and solely to denote pauses of different length irrespective of grammar and syntax. On the other hand the normal punctuation was much nearer to normal speech than is the case with our own, which balances one comma by another with a logic intolerable in talk. Thus the punctuation we find in the plays omits many stops which modern editors insert, and on the other hand inserts others, sometimes to mark the rhythm, sometimes to emphasize by a preliminary pause the word, or words which follow, sometimes for yet other reasons which can

OF SHAKESPEARE 91

hardly be enumerated. The only rule for dealing with these supra-grammatical stops, is to read the passage as punctuated, and then consider how it is affected by the pause at the point indicated. In the same way, if there is no stop where we expect one, or only a comma where we should expect a colon or even a full stop, we must try how the passage sounds with only light stops or none at all, and see what is the gain or loss to the dramatic impression.

As has already been admitted, the punctuation of most of the early Quartos, even when the system on which it is based is very liberally interpreted at the risk of turning faults into sham beauties, is inadequate and defective. But two points seem to emerge from the study of almost any early Quarto we take up. In the first place it seems clear that the value of all the stops was greater than at present. The comma is often used where we should put a semicolon; the semicolon for a colon; the colon for a full stop; while a full stop is a very emphatic stop indeed. If an Elizabethan printer had been given a typical passage of Macaulay to punctuate, he would have replaced many of his famous full stops by colons and some by commas. In such a case, where each sentence was grammatically complete in itself, but all were directed to building up by accumulation a single effect, an Elizabethan would have regarded all the sentences as co-ordinate parts of a whole and would have refused (unless rhetoric suggested an advantage in seeming to pause between each for a reply) to separate them by any stop heavier than a colon. Moreover, if it were desired to indicate by punctuation the rapidity of invective or earnest pleading, commas would have been made to do the work. A full stop, except when a speech is completely finished, always means business—very often theatrical business: at the least a change of tone or of the person addressed; occasionally, a sob or a caress.

Our second point is that even when we make ample allowance for the greater value of each of the four stops, and for his own carelessness and that of the printers, there is good evidence that Shakespeare preferred a light to a heavy punctuation.

'Speake the speech I pray you as I pronounc'd it to you, trippingly on the tongue, but if you mouth it as many of our Players do, I had as li[e]ve the towne cryer spoke my lines.' So Hamlet exhorted the players who were to test his uncle's guilt, and so (the punctuation of the early Quartos suggests) he may often have exhorted the actors at the Globe. In the 1604 Quarto of *Hamlet* the thirty-three lines of the speech that begins 'To be or not to be,' are punctuated with commas, two semicolons and a colon. The full stop only comes before the words: 'Soft you now The faire Ophelia.'

In Portia's famous speech in the *Merchant of Venice* there is a full stop after the plea that mercy

becomes
The thronèd Monarch better then his crowne

so that the idea may work its full effect before being followed by the gloss: 'His scepter shewes the force of temporall power,' etc. But after this, for thirteen lines there is no other full stop until the appeal is ended, and with a change of tone the pleader resumes:

I have spoke thus much
To mitigate the justice of thy plea,
Which if thou follow this strict court of Venice
Must needs give sentence gainst the Merchant here.

OF SHAKESPEARE 93

These particular punctuations are not held up for special admiration. It is in no way the business of bibliography to decide how Shakespeare's play should be punctuated. But when we find this notably light punctuation in editions of several different plays, set up by several different printers, it seems a fair bibliographical deduction that this light punctuation, though the printers may have corrupted it grossly, yet reflects a light punctuation in their copy, and so, immediately or by one or more removes, suggests what was Shakespeare's own habit.

We can make a similar deduction as regards the use of emphasis capitals, which may be taken to have indicated a slight exaltation in the tone in which the words they prefix were to be pronounced. In the early Quartos we find them used for titles of honour and respect, for abstract qualities and in metaphors; elsewhere only sparingly, and hardly ever in such a way as to encourage an actor to tear a passion to tatters. Thus in a speech which lies so exposed to over-emphasis as that of the Ghost in *Hamlet* beginning: 'Aye, that incestuous, that adulterate beast,' in the Quarto of 1604 there are only ten capitals, and these with two exceptions (Hebona and Lazerlike), merely follow the ordinary rules. Thus we find capitals assigned to Queen (twice), Crown, Uncle, Angel, Glowworm, Orchard and Denmark, and these are all, though the speech runs to just fifty lines. In the First Folio, on the other hand, there are just fifty emphasis capitals, or on an average one to every line, among the words emphasised being Beast, Traitorous, Lust, Lewdness, Garbage, etc., so that if an actor, when thus encouraged, resisted the temptation to mouthing, his grace was the greater

THE IMPROVERS

'In the very torrent tempest, and as I may say, whirlwind of your passion, you must acquire and beget a temperance, that may give it *smoothness*,' Hamlet tells the players, and bibliography may be permitted once more to quote this corroboration of its deduction that Shakespeare's manuscript was only moderately sprinkled with capitals.

III. The comparison that has just been made between the practice of the Quarto and Folio text of *Hamlet* in this matter of emphasis capitals brings us to the last point to be made in these papers, the point that, at least for some plays, the Folio must be regarded as an *edited* text, perhaps to about the same extent and in much the same manner as the Ellesmere manuscript of Chaucer's *Canterbury Tales* deserves that character. The Ellesmere scribe had ideas of his own on spelling and other matters, and a tendency if he did not find a verse smooth to leave it so. We have seen how ready someone was to smooth out lines in the First Folio. Probably he was doing the best thing for the book and its author that at that particular moment it was possible to do. Nor is it reasonable to be scornful if actors, who were responsible for bringing together the copy, took it for granted that the acting-versions then in use were the best possible, tolerated small verbal changes in the text, and thought it good if emphasis-capitals and punctuation were in accordance with the dramatic customs of their own day, rather than imperfect memoranda of Shakespeare's views.

How far the editing extended is a question of detail, from which the bibliographer must needs hold aloof. It has been noted already that the general editors of the Folio quickly tired of their task, and

OF SHAKESPEARE 95

perhaps the hired men who we believe to have collated and copied at the playhouse and the press-corrector in Jaggard's office may have tired also. It is possible also, and if human nature be taken into account, even probable, that when the copy arrived in manuscript and not in the form of a previously printed text, the craving to alter did not make itself felt in so severe a form. It could hardly have been otherwise than intensely interesting if Dr Aldis Wright, when fresh from revising the Cambridge Shakespeare, or Dr Howard Furness the elder, when in the full swing of work, had been tempted into a discussion as to whether the 'textus receptus' of the plays printed for the first time in the Folio of 1623 is better on an average, or worse, than in the case of plays of which a good Quarto as well as the Folio is available.

The literary side of editing a bibliographer must leave to his betters. Our task has been rescuing certain Quartos from most unbibliographical denunciations. We have quoted one wise and one not-so-wise remark from Dr Johnson's introduction to his edition of Shakespeare. It is amusing to find that Johnson in the prospectus which preceded by nine years the publication of his text out-heroded Herod in the vigour of his language. Here is what he wrote:

> The business of him that republishes an ancient book is, to correct what is corrupt, and to explain what is obscure. To have a text corrupt in many places, and in many doubtful, is, among the authors that have written since the use of types, almost peculiar to Shakespeare. Most writers, by publishing their own works, prevent all various readings and preclude all conjectural criticism. Books indeed are sometimes published after the death of

him who produced them, but they are better secured from corruptions than these unfortunate compositions. They subsist in a single copy, written or revised by the author; and the faults of the printed volume can be only faults of one descent.

But of the works of Shakespeare the condition has been far different; he sold them, not to be printed, but to be played. They were immediately copied for the actors, and multiplied by transcript after transcript, vitiated by the blunders of the penman, or changed by the affectation of the player; perhaps enlarged to introduce a jest, or mutilated to shorten the representation; and printed at last without the concurrence of the author, without the consent of the proprietor, from compilations made by chance or by stealth out of the separate parts written for the theatre; and thus thrust into the world surreptitiously and hastily, they suffered another depravation from the ignorance and negligence of the printers, as every man who knows the state of the press in that age will readily conceive.

It is not easy for invention to bring together so many causes concurring to vitiate a text. No other author ever gave up his works to fortune and time with so little care; no books could be left in hands so likely to injure them, as plays frequently acted, yet continued in manuscript; no other transcribers were likely to be so little qualified for their task, as those who copied for the stage, at a time when the lower ranks of the people were universally illiterate: no other Editions were made from fragments so minutely broken, and so fortuitously re-united; and in no other age was the art of printing in such unskilful hands.

It is curious that when Johnson wrote the sentence: 'It is not easy for invention to bring together so many causes concurring to vitiate a text,' he should not have paused to ask himself how many of his confident statements were based upon any kind of evidence and for how many a faculty not very distinct from that of invention might be held responsible. The theory that the plays must have been 'multiplied by transcript after transcript' has held the field from his day to our own and has not one shred of evidence to support it, nothing but an imaginative pessimism convinced that this is what must have happened. The statement that the plays were 'fragments minutely broken, fortuitously reunited' printed 'from compilations made by chance, or by stealth out of the separate parts written for the theatre' is on no higher level. Indeed it may be questioned whether for once in his life the great Doctor did not descend in this passage to writing sheer nonsense. That the plays might have been 'compilations made by *stealth* out of the separate parts written for the theatre' is conceivable, though there is no evidence to support it; but that these compilations could have been made by *chance*, that the fragmentary 'parts' could have been '*fortuitously* reunited' is surely not even conceivable, unless indeed the theatrical 'parts' of those days were fitted with legs and we are to understand that they danced themselves together in some order of their own devising.

It is only fair to Dr Johnson to remember that he wrote this Prospectus before he edited his author, and that in his Introduction after nine years' experience he writes nothing in this vein, though it seems clear that he pinned his faith with much too absolute confidence to the First Folio. The quotation from his Prospectus is only given here because it expresses with vigorous rhetoric about the worst view of the Quartos that even invention can dictate. As a contrast with it we may quote the much saner views

THE IMPROVERS

of Malone in his Introduction to the Shakespeare of 1790. He there writes:

Fifteen of Shakespeare's plays were printed in quarto antecedent to the first complete collection of his works, which was published by his fellow comedians in 1623... The players when they mention these copies, represent them all as mutilated and imperfect; but this was merely thrown out to give an additional value to their own edition and is not strictly true of any but two of the whole number; *The Merry Wives of Windsor*, and *King Henry V*. —With respect to the other thirteen copies, though undoubtedly they were all surreptitious, that is, stolen from the playhouse, and printed without the consent of the author or the proprietors, they *in general* are preferable to the exhibition of the same plays in the folio; for this plain reason, because, instead of printing these plays from a manuscript, the editors of the folio, to save labour, or from some other motive, printed the greater part of them from the very copies which they represented as maimed and imperfect, and frequently from a late, instead of the earliest, edition; in some instances with additions and alterations of their own. Thus therefore the first folio, as far as respects the plays above enumerated, labours under the disadvantage of being at least a second, and in some cases a third, edition of these quartos. I do not, however, mean to say, that many valuable corrections of passages undoubtedly corrupt in the quartos are not found in the folio copy; or that a single line of these plays should be printed by a careful editor without a minute examination and collation of both copies; but those copies were in general the basis on which the folio editors built, and are entitled to our particular attention and examination as *first* editions.

It is well known to those who are conversant with the business of the press, that, (unless when the author corrects and revises his own works,) as editions of books are multi-

OF SHAKESPEARE

plied their errors are multiplied also;...The various readings found in the different impressions of the quarto copies are frequently mentioned by the late editors: it is obvious from what has been already stated, that the first edition of each play is alone of any authority [except, he notes, in the case of *Romeo and Juliet*], and accordingly to no other have I paid any attention. All the variations in the subsequent quartos were made by accident or caprice. Where, however, there are two editions printed in the same year, or an undated copy, it is necessary to examine each of them, because which of them was first cannot be ascertained; and being each printed from a manuscript, they carry with them a degree of authority to which a reimpression cannot be entitled. Of the tragedy of *King Lear* there are no less than three copies varying from each other, printed for the same bookseller, and in the same year. Of all the plays of which there are no quarto copies extant, the first folio, printed in 1623, is the only authentick edition.

So far Malone, and if we have got beyond him in some points, in others, notably in his clear recognition that the Quartos 'were in general the basis on which the folio editors built,' and that (with stated exceptions) 'the first edition of each play is alone of any authority —all the variations in the subsequent Quartos were made by accident or caprice'—he is admirably sound.

What are the points in which we can claim to have got beyond Malone after a century and a quarter of further work? Not so many, it must be confessed, nor so important, as they should be. One or two new Quartos have been discovered, notably the *Hamlet* of 1603, giving a botched text of the play in its earlier form. We also know that there were only two early Quartos of *King Lear*, the belief that there were more being due to the co-existence in the first edition of uncorrected and corrected sheets such as those in *Richard II*, mentioned in our third paper.

So far as editors of Shakespeare are concerned it is doubtful whether their improvements on Malone can be shown to extend beyond these small points, and on the other hand they have hardly kept to his canon that only first editions can count as authorities. Quite recently, however, the three cases, the *Merchant of Venice*, the *Midsummer Night's Dream* and *King Lear*, in which the existence of two different editions bearing the same date led Malone to suppose that each was derived from a separate manuscript, have been resolved into three original editions, two of 1600 and one of 1608, and three reprints, all produced in 1619, and there is no longer any reason to believe in their being derived from rival manuscripts. It is rather strange that Malone did not make this discovery himself. Half a discoverer's work is done for him when the subject for investigation is rigidly isolated, and in Malone's day there must have been in existence nearly a dozen nice fat volumes, each containing the same nine plays, three of them, viz., the *Midsummer Night's Dream, Merchant of Venice* and *Sir John Oldcastle*, dated 1600; two others, *Henry V* and *King Lear*, dated 1608; three, the *Merry Wives of Windsor, Yorkshire Tragedy* and *Pericles*, dated 1619; and one, *The whole Contention between the two famous houses of York and Lancaster*, undated. One after another of these fat little volumes got broken up for convenience of sale or handling, and now, as far as is known, the only extant copy is that bearing the name of Edward Gwynn stamped on its cover, which after a long sojourn in Germany was brought back to England in 1902, sold through Quaritch to Mr Marsden Perry at Providence, Rhode Island and passed in 1919 into the possession of Mr Folger of New York on the basis of a catalogue price of no less than $100,000. Chance, however, brought this in 1902, and in 1906 a similar volume from the Hussey collection, under the same pair of eyes, and though the Hussey volume was broken up while a wild search was being made for a note of the contents of the fellow to it seen four years before, suspicion had at last been aroused, and the unravelment of the problem became only a question of time. Traces of similar volumes were found in the Capell collection at Trinity College, in the Garrick plays at the British Museum and elsewhere, and a first hypothesis was formed, that the plays with the earlier dates, four of them duplicating another edition of the same year, had sold badly and in 1619 were being made up into a volume with those printed in that year, as a kind of 'remainder.' Then Dr W. W. Greg made a spring at the true explanation, that the plays were all printed together in 1619, and proceeded to prove it by the very pretty, but very intricate evidence of the water-marks. After this the quarry was in full view and it was easy to hunt it down by a variety of proofs, the *coup de grâce* being given by an American student, Mr William Neidig, who showed photographically that the types used for the words 'Written by W. Shakespeare,' which occur on the three title-pages dated 1619, and also on that of the *Merchant of Venice* dated 1600, had remained untouched in the forme while all four titles were being printed—which could hardly have happened if they were separated by an interval of nineteen years.

The most lenient explanation of the five false dates assumes an original intention to prefix a general title-page to the collection, there being other instances of the short imprints and dates of first editions being placed on the separate title-pages of a volume of reprints by way of acknowledgement of the source and ownership of the text. The matter is complicated, however, by an apparent desire to establish a claim to two copyrights, those of the *Merchant of Venice* and *Midsummer Night's Dream*, which may have seemed to be derelict. For our present purpose, however, it suffices to note that the controversies as to which of the rival editions of these plays and of *King Lear* should be considered the earlier have been decisively settled in favour of those bearing the fuller imprints, and that it will be almost impossible for any future editor to maintain, as has hitherto been the fashion, that the falsely dated editions were printed from separate manuscripts. It seems quite clear that they must have been reprinted from the correctly dated First Editions, and that the variants in the text all originated in the printing-house.

The second point in which we claim to have improved on Malone is as to the interpretation to be placed on the oft-quoted words:

where (before) you were abus'd with diuerse stolne and surreptitious copies, maimed and deformed by the frauds and stealthes of iniurious impostors, that expos'd them: euen those, are now offer'd to your view cur'd and perfect of their limbes.

Malone, though he distinguished between the bad Quartos, such as those of the *Merry Wives of Windsor* and *King Henry V*, the texts of which were entirely rejected by the editors of the Folio, and the good

OF SHAKESPEARE

Quartos, which the Folio editors, either (as he supposes) 'to save labour or from some other motive,' used as their text in reprinting the plays, nevertheless says categorically:

Undoubtedly they were *all* surreptitious, that is stolen from the playhouse, and printed without the consent of the author or the proprietors.

It is confidently submitted that this assertion needlessly extends and enlarges the statement of the editors of the Folio, at the cost of making them decry their own property and tell foolish and gratuitous lies.

There is some slight ambiguity about the exact meaning of the word 'where' in the Preface to the First Folio. It is at least possible that it should be construed as equivalent to 'in those cases in which,' 'where before you were abus'd'—'in those cases in which you were abus'd'—'with diuerse stolne and surreptitious copies, even those are now offer'd to your view cur'd.' It is more probable, however, that it should be taken as meaning 'whereas'—whereas before you were abused, even those copies are now set right. Adopting this as the meaning less favourable to our case, may we not reasonably ask whether, if the players had intended to affix the charge of surreptitiousness on all the Quartos, they would have been content with so guarded a statement? Divers stolen and surreptitious copies had been issued—the first *Romeo and Juliet*, *Henry V*, the *Merry Wives*, the first *Hamlet*, probably a first *Loves Labors Lost*, which has not come down to us. All these editions had been rejected by the Folio editors, who had replaced them by good texts, and could therefore, without reference to any other texts, truthfully say— 'even those are now offer'd to your view cur'd and perfect of their limbes.'

IMPROVERS OF SHAKESPEARE

It is possible, of course, that when they mentioned 'diuerse copies' the Folio editors intended their readers to add the mental comment 'to wit, all the seventeen plays that have hitherto been printed.' But if they wanted this to be understood, why did they not say so? They had plenty of picturesque language at their command! Why should we make the words 'diuerse copies' apply to any except the plays which the Folio editors rejected, which bear their own evidence of a disreputable origin, and were never regularly entered on the Stationers' Register? Why should we extend it to the plays which the Folio editors were actually using as the source of their text, and of which in some cases the copyrights were at that moment vested in some of the publishers of the Folio?

It has been the object of these papers to show that the Quartos regularly entered on the Registers of the Stationers' Company were neither stolen nor surreptitious. I have gone further than this by bringing together some little evidence that some at least of these editions may have been set up from Shakespeare's autograph manuscript, and have further dangled before my readers the hope that in some of these much vilified texts there may yet survive evidence of how Shakespeare meant some of his great speeches to be delivered. This is as far as bibliography can take us. The literary critics must be allowed their rights. But if, overstepping these, they raise the foolish old cry, 'all stolne and surreptitious,' I hope in future they will be received with the answering whoop, 'Printed from the author's autograph,' for which there is at least as much justification as the other, and I venture to think a good deal more.

INDEX

A B C and *Catechism in English*, privilege for, 16, 18, 38
Actors' names substituted for characters, 64 *sqq.*
Actors, Peter, King's Stationer, 19
Adams, Richard, fined, 21
Almanacs, monopoly for printing, 16
Arber, Dr, views as to formation of Stationers' Company, 10 *sqq.*
Ass-head, stage property in *Midsummer Night's Dream*, 66
Authors, payment of in Shakespeare's day, 18 *sq.*, 24 *sq.*, 26 *sqq.*

Barker, Christopher, on grant of Charter to Stationers, 10; his monopoly for Bible-printing, 16
Barwick, G. F., on restrictions on Spanish printing, 11
Bible-printing, monopoly in, 16 *sq.*
Birrell, Augustine, his *Seven Lectures on Copyright* quoted, 5 *note*
Blount, E., employed to block piracies of Shakespeare's plays, 51 *sq.*
Boas, F. S., on the plays in Egerton MS. 1994, 57 *note*
Book-licences, how granted, 21 *sqq.*
Book-trade, regulation in the sixteenth century, 1–25
Buc, Sir George, his endorsements on plays, 58, 67
Burby, Cuthbert, an authorised publisher of Shakespeare's plays, 48 *sqq.*
Busby, J., pirates Shakespeare's plays, 41, 49 *sq.*

Capell, E., his readiness to accept unauthoritative readings which 'improve' Shakespeare's text, 86 *sqq.*; his copy of the volume of 1619, ix
Capitals, use of for emphasis in Shakespeare Quartos and First Folio, 97 *sq.*
Catechism in English, Day's monopoly for printing, 16, 18, 38
Caxton, W., not attacked by book-pirates, 1 *sq.*
Chamberlain's Men, 36, 44, 49 *sqq.*, 55 *sq.*
Chaucer, G., his works published at joint risk of four stationers,

20; old or modern spellings in, 87; Ellesmere MS. compared with First Folio, 94
Clergy, Elizabethan, payment of, 24 sq.
Complutensian Polyglot, issue delayed by privilege for Erasmus's Greek Testament, 3
Copyright, early history of in England, 1-34
Curll, Edmund, his literary piracies, 28, 33

Daborne, W., dramatist, made his own fair copies, 56; but *Poore Man's Comfort*, attributed to him, not in his autograph, 59
Danter, John, driven to literary piracy by need, 40, 48 sq.
Dating of books, ordered by Henry VIII, 7
Day, John, monopoly in *A B C* and *Catechism in English*, 16; a Stringer, 20; fined by Stationers' Company, 21
Dryden, John, his literary earnings prior to the first Copyright Act, 33

Edward VI, his proclamation on printing, 8
Elizabeth, Queen, policy as to printing, 12 sqq.; unrewarded dedication to, 27
Erasmus, D., his Greek Testament 'privileged,' 3

Faques, W., King's printer, 19
First Folio of Shakespeare's Plays, instances of guesswork in, 73 sq.; its good readings sometimes not derived from new MS., but from prompter's corrections on printed prompt copy, 79 sq.; the only one of the Four Folios of any importance, 83 sq.; yet itself an 'edited' text, 94 sq.
Fleay, F. G., his strange theory how *Romeo and Juliet* was pirated, 39
Fulke, Dr, payment for his confutation of the Rhemish Testament, 24

Garrick, D., his copy of the volume of 1619, ix
Glapthorne, H., his play *The Lady Mother*, 58
Goodale, T., his name in play of *Sir Thomas More*, 58
Googe, B., publication of his *Eglogs and Epytaphes*, 29 sq.
Grafton, R., privileges for service books, 16; a Grocer, 20
Greg, W. W., his theory how the *Merry Wives of Windsor* was pirated, 39; on Ant. Munday's handwriting, 59; his proof of false dates in Shakespeare Quartos, ix sq., 101

INDEX

Gwynn, Edward, his copy of the volume of 1619, viii

Hall, W., dealer in literary MSS., 31
Hamlet's advice to the players, applicable to punctuation and capitals in Shakespeare's text, 93 *sq.*
Heming and Condell, their editorial statements on the First Folio, 60 *sqq.*
Henry VIII, proclamations about printing, 5 *sqq.*
Henslowe, P., dealings with Daborne, 56
Herbert, Sir Henry, licenses *Lancheinge of the Mary*, 57; remits fee, 67
Heyes, Tho. and Laur., copyright in the *Merchant of Venice*, xii *note*
Heywood, T., his evidence as to piracy of plays, 38; his play *The Captives*, 58 *note*
'Hired men' in theatres possible pirates, 40
Horman, W., his *Vulgaria* privileged, 3
Huth, Alfred, *On the Supposed False Dates in certain Shakespeare Quartos*, x

Injunctions, Elizabethan, fifty-first on printing, 13 *sq.*, 16

Jaggard, Wm., on the watermarks in the volume of 1619, xii
James I, his example may have weakened fashionable prejudice against publication, 34
Johnson, S., views on construction of Shakespeare's text, 83; scorns punctuation of the early Quartos, 89 *sq.*; extravagant depreciation of the Quarto texts, 95 *sqq.*
Jugge, R., Bible printing secured to, by Archbishop Parker, 16

King Lear, circumstances of its publication, 51 *sq.*, 99 *sq.*

Lambe, Sir J., his note as to book-licensing, 22
Lancheinge of the Mary, its autograph endorsed by licenser, 57
Lant, R., imprisoned by Stationers' Company, 21
Licensing of books, 21 *sqq.*; of plays, endorsed on author's MS., 57 *sq.*, 67
Loves Labors Lost, a pirated edition probably lost, 47

Machlinia, W. de, reprints Caxton's *Chronicles of England*, 2, 4
Malone, Edmund, his estimate of the Shakespeare First Quartos, 98 *sqq.*

INDEX

Marshe, Thomas, held monopoly for printing Latin schoolbooks, 16

Mary, Queen, policy as to printing, 8 *sqq.*

Massinger, P., extant MS. of his *Believe as you List*, in his autograph, 57, 62

Mayors, books printed in a town to be deposited with, 7

Merchant of Venice, falsely dated edition, 43, 100 *sqq.*

Midsummer Night's Dream, falsely dated edition, 43, 100 *sqq.*; Q^1 contains a revised text, xxv

Millar v. *Taylor*, copyright case quoted, 4 *note*

Milton, John, contract for payment for *Paradise Lost* prior to the first Copyright Act, 33

Mountford, William, his *Lancheinge of the Mary*, 57

Munday, Anthony, plays in his autograph, 57

Nashe, T., dedication to *The Terrors of the Night*, quoted, 32

Neidig, W., photographic proof of false dates in Shakespeare Quartos, xi *sq.*, 101

Pace, Richard, privilege granted in 1518 for his sermon on Peace, 3

Pamphlet, payment for writing in Shakespeare's day, 24, 36

Parker, Archbishop, kept Bible-printing in Jugge's hand, 16

Patronage, effect of on author's earnings, 27 *sq.*

Pembroke and Montgomery, Earls of, servility of dedication of First Folio to, 60

Percy, W., publication of his *Sonnets to Coelia*, 30

Perry, Marsden, purchaser of the only unbroken copy of the 1619 volume of Shakespeare Quartos, 101

Piratical printing, precautions against, 23; extent of in Shakespeare's day, 32 *sqq.*

Place of printing, ordered by Henry VIII to be stated in books, 8

Plays, Elizabethan payments for, 36; selling value, 37; possible methods of pirating, 39 *sqq.*; entry on Stationers' Register *prima facie* evidence of authenticity, 48; of Shakespeare's time, extant in author's autograph, 57 *sq.*

Pope, A., his shifts to get his letters printed, 28

Printers, when first admitted to the Stationers' Company, 20

Printing, subjection to Government control, 5 *sqq.*; avoided by fashionable Elizabethans, 27–33

Priuilegium ad imprimendum solum, meaning of phrase, 6 *sq.*

# INDEX

Privileges for book-printing, 2–4; for exclusive rights in classes of books, 16 sq.
Privy Council, its control of printing, 8, 13, 17 sqq., 34; its relation to the players, 35 sqq.
Proclamations on printing, 5 sqq.
Prohibited books, English lists of, 5
Prompt-copies, author's autograph used for, subsequently printed, 64 sqq.
Prompter's notes, survival of, in printed texts, 64 sqq.
Provinces, printing in the, 13
Punctuation in first Quartos of Shakespeare's plays may be authoritative, xix sqq., 91 sqq.
Pynson, R., privilege granted to books printed by, 3; whether a stationer, 19; his assessment, 20

Quartos of Shakespeare's plays, used as prompt-copies and subsequently for First Folio, 66 sq.; the blunders in them, 69 sqq.; corrected and uncorrected sheets in same edition, 70 sq.; no fresh MS. consulted for later Quartos, 72 sq.; the First Quartos alone authoritative, 83 sqq.; may retain some of Shakespeare's own punctuation, 89 sqq.; Malone's estimate of them only marred by repetition of charge of surreptitiousness, 98–102; the false dates in the 1619 reprints, 100 sqq.; the charge of surreptitiousness reckless, 103 sqq.

Reformation, effect of in subjecting printing to control, 5, 23
Richard II, badness of Second Quarto, 69; variations in copy of First Quarto, 70, 82 *note*
Roberts, James, enters plays on Stationers' Register to defeat pirates, xiii, 43 sq.
Robinson, R., his literary earnings, 24, 27
Romeo and Juliet, Fleay's theory as to its piracy, 39

Schoolmasters, Elizabethan, payments of, 24 sq.
Scriveners, Nashe's grudge at their profits, 32
Secret presses, fewness of, under Elizabeth, 15
Shakespeare, W., only two of his sonnets pirated during 15 years, 31; the attempts to pirate his plays, 39–52; the transmission of his text from manuscript to Quartos and Folio, 53–80; treatment of, by editors, 81–102
Sidney, Sir Henry and Philip, gift for a dedication, 27

INDEX

Simpson, Percy, his treatise on Shakespearian punctuation, xv, 90

Sir Thomas More, play of, Shakespeare's hand in, xxiii, 58

Spain, restrictions on printing in, 11

Stage-directions, two kinds of, 63 *sqq.*

Star Chamber, its limitation of presses partly directed to securing a livelihood for existing printers, 17 *sq.*, 34

Stationers, wealthier than early printers, 20

Stationers' Company, grant of charter to, 9 *sqq.*; its early history, 19–25

Stationers' Register, method of entering books on, 21–23; entry *prima facie* evidence of authority, 48 *sqq.*, 104

Stenography, used in pirating plays, 38

Taverner, J., stationer, his wealth, 20

Tawyer with a trumpet, in stage-directions, 66

Theobald, L., appraisal of editions of Shakespeare, 82 *sqq.*

Thiselton, A. E., a pioneer in explaining Shakespearian punctuation, 90

Thorpe, T., dealer in literary MSS., 31 *sq.*

Tottell, R., his privilege for law-books, 16 *sq.*

Troilus and Cressida, circumstances of its publication, 50 *sqq.*

Venice, privileges for books first given at, 2

Ward, R., attacks privileged printers, 17

Watkins, R., monopoly in English almanacs, 16

Whitchurch, E., privileges for service books, 16; a haberdasher, 20

Wilson, J. Dover, on 'the Lunatic, the Lover and the Poet' in *Midsummer Night's Dream*, xxv

Wilson, Jack, his name in stage directions, 66

Wither, George, his charges against the Stationers, 25, 33

'Within,' use of, in stage directions, 65

Wolfe, John, attacks privileged printers, 17

www.ingramcontent.com/pod-product-compliance
Lightning Source LLC
Chambersburg PA
CBHW061328040426
42444CB00011B/2812